Cuckoo Pounds and Singing Barrows

The Folklore of Ancient Sites
in Dorset

Jeremy I

GW00566746

Dorset Natural History & Archaeological Society

1986

1

Published by the Dorset Natural History & Archaeological Society, Dorset County Museum, Dorchester, Dorset DT1 1XA

Typeset by Shaun Ryan Typesetting, Suite E, Georgian House, Dorchester, Dorset

Printed by Yeoprint, 13/14 Wyndham Street, Yeovil, Somerset

Mansel-Playdell Prize Essay 1984

Harte, Jeremy
    Cuckoo pounds and singing barrows:
    the folklore of Dorset's archaeology
    1. Folklore — England — Dorset
    I. Title
    398'.094223'3   GR142.D6
    ISBN 0 900341 23 8

CONTENTS

Spetisbury Rings as seen by John Baverstock Knight (1783-1859), with Crawford Cross in the foreground.

TRADITION

Archaeology began with folklore, and developed from popular traditions into an academic discipline. It is easy to forget that sites like Maiden Castle, Knowlton, or the Nine Stones were not 'discovered' by the antiquarians of the 16th and 17th centuries: they were shown to them by a peasantry who had long been familiar with the sites, and who had developed theories and beliefs to account for them. Folklore is a kind of knowledge suited to casual curiosity, passed on by word of mouth or through ephemeral publications, and subject always to the gently stereotyping influence of the popular imagination. For every archaeologist searching for truth by excavation, there are a dozen indifferent bystanders whose ideas, if they are expressed at all, still run on the old themes of buried treasures, graves from forgotten wars, spectres, and ancient wisdom. The study of archaeological folklore, at one time and another, has been too highly praised or too little valued. No-one would now claim, with the Victorian anthropologists, that the traditions of the rural working class preserve real memories from prehistory: our knowledge of how fast tradition can grow, and how easily it will change, does not allow this. But to regard the legends of pre-historic and Roman monuments as merely curiosities or popular fancies to discard potential source of evidence, which in its own way may be as valid as aerial photography or resistivity surveys (and is also cheaper). The successive generations that worked the land had time to notice those slight earthworks, hollows of rich soil, and obstructive remnants of walls, which otherwise would be concealed from all but the closest fieldwork. Their observations may be wrapped up in legends, but they give a good indication on where to look for facts. In the case of known and obvious archaeological sites, folklore itself may be a layer of their history; if the lowest stratum is a henge or hillfort, the uppermost may reveal fairground debris, the ashes of a beacon or bonfire, or the relics of an annual festival. These are as important for history as the original layers, just as the ideas associated with ancient monuments are as worthy of record as material finds from excavation. It is neglectful to go sifting the evidence for Bronze Age superstition at a barrow, and not to spend an evening at the pub collecting its modern equivalent.

As a rule, folk memory goes back for three centuries but loses interest in any earlier date. The stock of legends in modern Dorset includes some based on the Monmouth Rising, exactly three hundred years ago, but these are beginning to slide out of popular memory, to be replaced by tales of the 18th-century wrecks and wreckers, smuggling, and the defence against Napoleon. Similarly, looking back at earlier collections of folklore, we find that legends about Athelstan, the great king of Wessex and of England who died in 940, lasted into the time of William of Malmesbury when he wrote in 1120 and were used in about 1230 to account for the chapel at Milton Abbas. Stories of the Wars of the Roses were current when Michael Drayton wrote his *Polyolbion* in 1613. Both these topics have now vanished from folk memory, and it is unreasonable to expect that folklore should hold onto traditions from an earlier, prehistoric date. This is not to deny that certain *types* of legend or customs go back to a very early date; as we shall see, much of the folklore of Dorset's ancient monuments represents themes which have belonged to.people of all times and places; but such continuity is of general patterns of folklore, not of individual, local traditions.It is easy for a generally known custom or story to become attached to a partic-ular monument and then (within only a few years) get accepted as something immemorially old. Examples are given in the Inventory, such as fairs at Poundbury and the May day dancing at Cerne.

So where local folklore refers to an early period, and speaks of Roman or prehistoric times, it is probably not so much an inherited tradition as a kind of folk archaeology. Country people are as capable of making deductions from monumental evidence as the experts: after all, the first reference to crop-marks comes not from the antiquaries, but from a Wiltshire tradition, recorded by Aubrey; St. Thomas Becket's Path was to be seen across some village fields when the corn was ripe (Aubrey 1687 p245). Similar observations were part of communal history. At a village which I take to be Lockerly (Hants.) – it is pseudonymous in the text – open field strips were still recognised as shadow patterns in the 20s. 'One January afternoon, the sun was low, just level with the top of the church; the winter shadows light, and long. Father looked in, and said to me . . . "You look close at the sward, my boy. You see those dips? You can only see 'em certain times when the light and the sun is like it is now. They don't run straight, look – they run in a great double curve, like an S turned round backwards . . .And if you look between them dips," went on my father, "you'll see lines of darker grass, that follows them curves down – like strips. Do you see that?"

'The pattern revealed itself. I wondered why I had not noticed it before.

' "Well," went on my father, "if you count them strips from the coppice yonder, the first five used to belong to your great-great-grandfather' " (Goodland 1967 p128).

This kind of observation, combined with a little historical knowledge, will explain the placenames referring to Romans at archaeological sites. In 1965, J. Bailey found a pit of Romano-British household rubbish in Litton Cheney (SY 55369080),* implying the existence of a house nearby, though this was not found. 'The discovery of this pit is of special interest, since some 150 yards away there is a spring known locally as 'Roman Well'. Unfortunately the area between the spring and the pit is covered with houses, making further investigation almost impossible' (*DP* 87p91, 1965). Likewise a field called Tombstone Acre in Portland turned out to contain traces of Romano-British occupation (*DP* 76p75, 1954). There are some close parallels to this from Somerset. An orchard at Melbury near Somerton contained a well known in 1924 as the Roman Well, and twenty-five years later excavation discovered a Roman building in the orchard (*SDNQ* 25p238,49). Earlier, in 1900, a Roman villa was uncovered at Brislington, where no Roman site had been previously expected, 'with the exception that this identical field was known locally as the 'Roman Paddock' '(*SDNQ* 7p27, 1900).

Similar evidence for this kind of folk archaeology comes from field names like *Walls* and *Castle*, given to places where two or three centuries ago ancient remains were to be seen. The increased appetite of the plough has destroyed everything above ground, but the name remains, and can be used as a clue for the archaeologist. The field called Walls on the Shapwick Tithe Map of 1848 lies near the Roman villa at Hemsworth. A villa was excavated at Walls Field in Charminster (*DP* 82p86, 1960), and this prompted C. J. Bailey to investigate a field, first recorded as Walls in 1791, in Puncknowle; he found an extensive Romano-British settlement (*DP* 87p90, 1965). It would be premature to think of *Walls* as a name specifically for villas, since (as we shall see) a field in Ilminster uses the name for 17th-century ruins, but the placename is one that calls for investigation. A field in Wyke Regis occurs as Wall Mead in 1816 (DRO:D519/T5) and Wall Close on the Tithe Map of 1841. There is a Walls Down at 593.830 in Abbotsbury, on Taylor's map of 1765; the 1887 OS shows Wall Farm at 425.014 in Stoke Abbot. Wallis Farm in Frome Vauchurch (594.990) and Wallsend Cove on Portland (67.69) should be noted, though their derivation is probably different.

Chesil (from OE *ceosol*, 'gravel'), is another name associated with Roman sites (Hoskins 1963 p93). There have been Roman finds from a field called Chisels in Shipton Gorge (*DP* 78p87, 1956).

---

* Future grid references will use only six figures and omit the initial letters ST, SU, SY or SZ, which are not needed for Dorset references.

The name *Castle* is frequently associated with prehistoric remains as well as mediaeval ones. The Saxon word for a defensive earthwork (old or new) was *burh*; this appears in modern placenames as the suffic *-bury*. At some date after the conquest, the meaning of *burh* was forgotten, and it was replaced in popular speech by the use of French *castel* or Latin *castellum*. Eggardon was a *castellum* in 1300, as appears from the Inventory, and Lambert's Castle is so called in the 15th century. *Castle* remains the ordinary term in western Dorset, as at Abbotsbury and Cattistock. *Castelwode* (1468) in Shapwick presumably lay near Badbury; Castle Close (1837) in Hampreston was by Dudsbury; Castle Mead (1803 – in DRO:D40H/T21) and Castle Lane in Okeford Fitzpaine must refer to Banbury. These names illustrate the fact that, until a few centuries ago, there was no real idea of prehistory. A hillfort was just an old castle, and a mediaeval earthwork was a new one. As late as the 17th century proposals were being made to refortify the old works in case of emergency; the art of war had not changed enough to make them obsolete.

From the 18th century onwards, with the disuse of castles of any sort, the term *rings* has been applied to ancient earthworks (not, except at Corfe Castle, to mediaeval ones). It is now becoming part of their ordinary names – even 'Maiden Castle Rings' occurs in local usage (*DYB* 1943-4p22), and everyone says Badbury Rings, Maumbury Rings, etc. The triple sequence is shown at Spetisbury, which was originally *spehtes burh*, the woodpeckers' fort. Hutchins records a mediaeval name, Crawford Castle: but already in his time this name was being replaced by Spettisbury Rings, the name in use today.

From this it follows that *castle* names may preserve the site of earthworks which were visible in the middle ages, and which are probably prehistoric. The Tithe Map for Wareham Holy Trinity (1843) shows a Castle Close in Arne.At Portland a 'close called Castles' occurs in 1608 and on the Tithe Map (1839); it is probably 'the place in Portland, the site of the Alexandra Inn . . . called Giants' Castle' (Waring 1977 p50). There was a *Castelcombe* in 1481 at Preston. Castle Farm and Hill in Lytchett Matravers appear on the 1811 OS and Tithe Map; the local historian F. Carré supposed an earthwork had stood here, but did not report any remains. Castle Hill in Puddletown, on the 1887 OS, stands by the Roman road, though no earthwork can be made out in the rough heathland. Castle Field appears on the Enclosure Map for Tarrant Crawford in 1809. And there is a Castle Barn at 714.100 in Pulham on the 1887 OS.

TREASURE

Few people, however, are inspired by a disinterested curiosity about the past. Excavation has always been interpreted as a search for treasure, and while the modern 'treasure-hunter' may be content with mediaeval coins and Victorian knick-knacks, folk tradition has always dreamed of gold. When General Pitt-Rivers was excavating in Cranborne Chase, popular rumour had it that he was looking for the golden coffin buried near Bridmore Green in Berwick St. John (Parke 1963 p481). There is a terser version of the belief from one of the General's old diggers: 'E'd a bin always lookin' vur King John's treasure' (*Dorset* 64p23, 1977). This fascination with golden coffins runs through the folklore of ancient sites in Wessex. In the present Inventory there are golden or silver coffins ascribed to Badbury, the Grey Mare, Hod Hill, Poor Lot, Thickthorn long barrow, Wilkwood and Wor Barrow, as well as an identification of a leaden Roman sarcophagus found at Winterbourne Kingston with its legendary counterpart. This instance suggests that golden coffin stories may develop from the findings of actual Roman burials. If this were so, one would expect a bias to Roman sites: but while the Badbury tradition can be interpreted as referring to the camp at Crab Farm, and there was Roman activity at Hod

Hill and Wor Barrow, the comparison with other counties shows that most golden coffin traditions belong to barrows. There have been golden coffins – Attila was buried in one – but the archaeological tradition is probably only the work of imagination. Eric Benfield reflected on the subject: 'I have never been able to discover even a hint of . . . how this story got started, yet casually a man or woman will still drop a word or two about it as lying in this wood or that garden . . .I have received a hint that it lies somewhere in the village of Worth and also in Downshay Wood, and in repeating it here . . . do it completely without embarassment, as I have great hopes that some day a great heavy golden coffin will be levered out of Dorset ground' (Benfield 1950 p158).

There are some traditions that only mention 'treasure', like that at the Bloxworth Down barrows and the earlier barrow-digging at Upwey. A ghost appeared as the guardian of a Roman coin hoard at Sixpenny Handley, and a dream revealed treasure –in the form of a Roman vase – at Witchampton. There seems to have been a particular preconception that treasure lay under Roman pavements, and this led to the destruction of mosaics at Halstock and Rampisham when they were discovered in the 18th century. The story is brought up to date by the bizarre incidents at Winterborne Houghton, where two enthusiasts for riddles started looking for Kit Williams' golden hare in a group of round barrows. They were of course breaking the law, and modern treasure-hunters should remember that gold belongs to the crown as treasure trove.

There are several sites which have treasure traditions without any corresponding monuments, and some of these tales may be of archaeological value. 'Tradition says there is a golden table at the bottom of a well' at Court Hill in Ryme Intrinseca, 'but none have been sufficiently curious to attempt to find it' (Dacombe 1935 p149). 'I have heard of a crock of gold at Caswell, which is virtually the same place' (Waring 1977 p72). 'There is a legend of a silver table that is said to be buried under some yew trees about half a mile from the village' at Tarrant Gunville (Palmer 1973 p149). 'In Culeaze at Milborne St. Andrew a golden coffin is said to be buried – and they do say that every time anyone goes to dig for it, it thunders and lightens' (Dacombe 1935 p106). An informant in 1983 told me that treasure from the Civil Wars is hidden in a tree in the Manor at Martinstown. The field now known as Golter in Langton Matravers was *Goldeherd Croft* in 1497, alluding to a 'Golden hoard', and likewise Gaulter Cottages in Steeple (908792) were *claus voc' Goldehorde* in 1451. Vaguest of all is the 'popular tradition that a treasure lies hidden in the earth somewhere between Weymouth and Purbeck Island' (Warne 1866 iii p10).

There are numerous Golden Valleys, Fields and Hills among Dorset placenames, but these appear, from their local situation, to be descriptions of the fertility of the soil rather than references to concealed hoards. The names, however, are still capable of inspiring folklore, as when in 1923 the Revd. G. Glenfield, a Methodist minister who had a reputation as a dowser, 'sensed precious metal' when passing over Gold Hill in Shaftes-bury. He received permission to excavate, but no treasure came to light, (*Dorset* 62p40, 1977).

The chief motive for these legends is the old lure of free riches, to be accidentally disinterred by the spade, which must have fortified generations of labourers – as it did one man reclaiming land in the Fitzworth peninsula (Corfe Castle) in the 50s. 'He told me that the only thing that kept him going, when he was driving fences across newly-won territory, was the notion that in the next post-hole he might strike the treasure that Harry Paye, Poole buccaneer and Vice-Admiral of the Cinque Ports, is reputed to have buried hereabouts in the early fifteeenth century. He never found it'. (Hyland 1978 p37). Some of the stories of treasure at barrows are probably based either on finds of Wessex Culture grave goods, or on the practice in classical times of burying hoards in old mounds – conspicuous landmarks from which the money could later be retrieved. A barrow in Tarrant Hinton (Grinsell's 5g) was found to contain 'a small Roman urn, filled with coins of Constantine, Constantius, and others of the same period; the hidden store of some Roman, or Romano-Briton, which had been deposited for concealment' (Hutchins 1861-70 1p318). And some have struck lucky with these Roman hoards. 'In the year 1816 . . . a carter of the name of Willshire, when ploughing in a field not half a mile distant from Rimbury [in Preston], turned up an urn filled with Roman coins . . . They numbered several hundreds, and were hawked about at an average price of one shilling each. Willshire's wife also regularly attended Weymouth market, with the coins exposed for sale in a plate on a standing. The proceeds formed a nucleus (small as it might have been), which was embarked in smuggling trans-actions, and proving successful (his sons being bold fellows), the condition of the family was materially improved; indeed one of the sons at the time of our excavations, was in the occupation of a farm of considerable extent in the adjoining village of Osmington' (Warne 1866 p60). Doubtless the same thing had happened before, unrecorded except in folklore; in Tongue 1967 p197, for instance, there is a traditional account of a Spaxton ploughman called Caddick who 'turned up a heap of money at the old Castle near Three Horshoes Hill above Aisholt – and when he went to the States he sold the coins there for a dollar each'. The value of such finds of treasure has decreased only in proportion to rising standards of living: if poverty were as sharp in modern Dorchester as it used to be, the Muckleford and Marks and Spencer hoards would have proved as serviceable as the Rimbury find.

BURIAL

Pagan burial was the oldest use made of prehistoric sites in Dorset. From the beginning of the sixth century, until the county was absorbed into Christian Wessex, it was a custom of the English in Dorset to bury their dead in the barrows and earthworks left by earlier civilisations. It is not altogether clear how many of these burials have been found, for they were usually interred without grave goods and even modern excavation cannot always distinguish them from the dead of earlier periods. There are about a dozen reliable instances, mostly coming from the area of Cranborne Chase.

At the north-east of the county a woman was buried in a barrow. Grinsell's Wimborne St. Giles 1, on Oakley Down. She wore a necklace made from mingled beads of amber, glass and bronze, and her clothes were fastened with a saucer-brooch of gilt bronze (Grinsell 1959). As in other instances further south, this barrow lay by what is now a parish boundary – it is a little way west of the Pentridge-Wimborne border – showing that the dividing line between estates was the same in the seventh century as it is now. Moreover, one of the estates has a Celtic name. Pentridge (*Pentric* 762) comes from *penn tyrch*, 'the hill of the wild boar'; this hill is the modern Penbury Knoll, crowned by a hillfort. The form of the word, with the noun preceding the adjective, dates it to a time after the sixth century, so that it was a relatively new name when the Saxon woman first heard it.

The long barrow Chettle I lies on the Chettle/Hinton border. When some desultory excavation took place here in the 18th century, burials with 'heads of spears and other warlike instruments' were disinterred at the side of the barrow, and a woman was found buried a foot beneath its summit (Hutchins 1861-70, 3, p569). A short way north-east of this site is Week Street Down, a name preserving the memory of a *vicus* which may have been a planned Saxon settlement; perhaps it lay by Gussage Hill, which appears in the Inventory under its earlier name of Seven Ditches.

9

Three barrows on the border of Long Crichel and Launceston have yielded Saxon burials. They were of a child, a man of about 18 and another man; the 18-year old had been buried with an iron knife and sheath, a bronze buckle and an iron awl (*DP* 104p57). Three more people were found in Long Crichel 19, and one in Long Crichel 22 was buried, contrary to the usual rite, in a crouched position (Piggott 1944 p69,71). Two Celtic placenames survive near these barrows; south of them are the trees of Chetterwood, which originally meant 'the ford in the wood', and immediately to the southeast is Crichel Hill. This landmark, from which the manors of More and Long Crichel take their name, is compounded from *crug* and *hyll* – two words, British and English, for the same thing.

At Knowlton Rings in 1938, C. M. Piggott observed a skeleton lying east and west on top of the Great Barrow. It had been exposed by rabbit workings, and so was obviously an intrusive burial close to the surface (Read 1947 p286). Later, in 1962, the section cut by a pipe-trench revealed more burials at three points. At about 024.102 six burials were exposed, and nine more were found near the Great Barrow, either within the southern edge of its surrounding ditch or by the eastern side of that ditch. Three of the burials were examined. They lay parallel to each other, and were of a man, a woman, and a child of about 11-14; the man had his arms crossed over his chest (DP 84p117,1962).

It appears that some of the monuments at Knowlton formerly lay on an estate border. The bounds of Cranborne Chase, as recorded in 1279, run north up the Allen and then turn off by a long hedge. They then go east along *le Muledich*, a linear earthwork with, running south by it, the access lane to a mill which must formerly have stood a little upstream of Bidcombe Bone Mill. From the *Muledich* the bounds come to the southernmost of the Knowlton Rings, where New Barn is now, then they circumvent *Knyges*, which Dayrell Read interpreted as the lands of Knoll Hill Farm; in his day these still bore the name of 'Kings'. From thence they run eastwards to the Crane (*DP* 53p215, 1931). Now, from Domesday Book we know that in 1086 the area of the modern parish of Woodlands comprised two manors – one belonging to the King and surveyed with other Royal estates (entry 1.16), and one held by Ansgar of the Count of Mortain (entry 26.43). Ansgar farmed a ploughland with one bordar and one slave; he had a mill, the rent from which (12/6d) amounted to half the value of the estate. This ploughland is evidently the fields north-west of the Chase boundary, and the bordar worked his mill at the end of the *Muledich*, while the King's land consisted of Knoll Hill Farm and the later clearing of Woodlands, lying south-east of the boundary line.

Burials which may be Saxon – they were extended and had no grave goods – have been found to the north-west and east of the Bradford Barrow (Pamphill 5), which may be Roman (*DP* 104p83, 1982). Not far away, Witchampton preserves the name of another *vicus*, and the Roman-British remains are extensive enough in this area near Badbury for the farm boundaries to be conjectured; if N. H. Field is right in this, three farms had a common border at the barrow.

Further west, burials have been found at the Steepleton enclosure – a Neolithic hilltop settlement on the ridge extending from Hambledon Hill. They lay at 855.115, near the Shroton/Hanford boundary, and were set into the bank (which then stood slightly above ground) on the inner side of a causewayed ditch. There were fourteen burials; two of them were of men buried with their knives, and one double grave had been dug for a man and a woman. There were two or three children among the burials (Mercer 1980 p53).

At another Neolithic site, the henge at Mount Pleasant, two burials have been found. An elderly man was buried with a knife and wearing a buckle on his clothing, by the ditch near the west entrance of the main enclosures; a young woman lay in the ditch which once surrounded the Neolithic timber structure (Wainwright 1979 p181). The western edge of Mount Pleasant, with Conquer Barrow on it, serves as a boundary between Fordington and West Stafford. Here too the association with Celtic placenames holds good, for a little way upstream the church of Frome Whitfield (now lost) lay in a field called Eglysham from *egles*, 'a church'. Evidently a Celtic-speaking community had kept up their institutions alongside the new Saxon colonists.

Maiden Castle has at least one Saxon burial. At the eastern end of the Neolithic long mound, just south of the Romano-British temple, a mature man was buried with his weapons, a scramasax and a small knife (Wheeler 1943 p78). The scramasax has been dated to the later 7th century (*DP* 90p238, 1968). There are two other burials in the long mound. A little west of the man with the scramasax lay another man, of about 30, who had been mutilated before burial with a sharp weapon, probably a sword; his arms and legs were hacked off the torso and the face wholly mutilated (*World Archaeology* 3ii p233, 1971). A radiocarbon dating (which has, however, been the subject of debate) suggested that the man died in about 635. Wheeler identified four burials further along the mound – extended with heads to the west – as Romano-British on the evidence of a pottery sherd in the infill of the grave; the possibility remains that they might be Saxon instead. At present the boundary of Monkton and Martinstown runs down the track from the A35, then loops around Maiden Castle on the eastern side, returns halfway along its southern face to a point below the entry of the legendary tunnel, and carries on south again. It looks very much as if it originally went straight over the fort, as had been the case at Abbotsbury, Shipton and Eggardon, in which case the parish boundary would have extended over the long mound.

Culliford Tree or Kings Barrow (Whitcombe 1), lying on the ridgeway south of Maiden Castle, may have served as the grave of a Saxon woman like that on Oakley Down. Barrow diggers of the last century found four burials near the surface of the mound, one of them wearing a necklace strung with amber beads; two of the beads were clasped in gold. The barrow lies on the Whitcombe/Came border, and Grinsell is inclined to interpret these burials as Saxon (Grinsell 1982).

In western Dorset, three burials laid out with their heads to the west have been found in a barrow which lies in an ancient enclosure on the ridge south of Eggardon. The enclosure, which must be on or near the Askerswell/Powerstock boundary, is undated but appears to be earlier than the hillfort (*DP* 104p181, 1982). Laurence Keen has kindly told me that these burials have been carbon-dated to c.750.

Finally, at Hardown Hill on the Whitchurch/Chideock boundary several burials were found in one of the barrows Whitchurch 1-6. No records were kept of the excavation, but since a brooch and nine spears survive from the finds, there must have been a woman and at least four or five men buried here. The brooch is of a kind made between 450 and 550 AD (*DP* 90p233, 1969). It is perhaps worth noting that the grave goods included a pebble (now lost) with a hole naturally bored through it, and that such pebbles have been kept as good-luck charms by modern fisherman on the coast here, from Burton and Abbotsbury down to Portland.

There is no doubt that these burials follow a consistent pattern. The bodies are laid out as we bury our dead today, extended and supine with their heads lying to the west (sometimes more towards the south-west); they lie a little way below the surface of mounds or in their surrounding ditches. Apart from barrows, these people made use of Neolithic monuments: Knowlton Rings and Mount Pleasant belong entirely to that period, while at Maiden Castle and the ridge near Hambledon Neolithic remains were used rather than the more imposing

Iron Age forts nearby. This apparent archaeological sophistication is probably the result of a desire to avoid hillforts which had once belonged to the ancestors of the native British population. As to date, the burials at Hardown Hill are the earliest; otherwise, judging from the dating of the Maiden Castle scramasax and the general paucity of grave goods, these people died in the seventh century. The *Anglo-Saxon Chronicle* records that Cenwalh, who reigned 643 – 672, mounted fresh campaigns against the British, one of which must have involved the annexation of Dorset. By 705, when Aldhelm was Bishop of Sherborne, the county passed under the civil and ecclesiastical authority of Wessex. The seventh-century pagans, then, were settlers in what was still an independent Celtic state; the proximity of their burials to surviving Celtic placenames bears this out. There is a striking concordance between the evidence of graves and words. Evidently the families buried near Pentridge, Crichel and Witchampton adopted those names from their British predecessors and handed them down to us. Since all the burials lie on boundaries of one sort or another, there must have existed a double system of interment – the Christian British using consecrated cemeteries adjoining their place of settlement, while their pagan English neighbours took their dead up to the ancient monuments which served as boundary markers between one estate and another.

There is one documentary reference to the custom of boundary burial. A Piddletrenthide charter of 966 includes in its landmarks the *Hathene Berielese*, 'heathen burial place'. According to Grundy's reading of the obscure boundary, this would have lain near the crossroads at 682.003, on the Cerne/Piddletrenthide border (*DP* 59p109, 1937). These heathens were presumably more pagan English of the seventh century, though considering the date they might perhaps be defeated members of a Viking raiding party. The latter explanation is suggested by *Hethenstrere* (1438) at Warmwell, where Mills proposes as one interpretation, 'road thought to have been used . . . by Danish marauders', the 'heathen' of the *Anglo-Saxon Chronicle*.

An analogous burial practice must have taken place at the sites whose names contain 'dead men' or something similar. Taking a view from north-east to south-west again, there are eleven of these places in Dorset. 'A bush called dead man's bush, where is a bound-stone that parteth Gillingham, Meere and Milton' was visited in a perambulation of the 17th century. It appears to have lain on the border of Gillingham in Dorset and Mere in Somerset, at 798.309 (*SDNQ* 17p93, 1921). Deadman's Coppice on the 1829 Enclosure Map for Ashmore appears as *Dead mans* in 1618. Deadman Field in Wimborne St. Giles is shown by the Tithe Map of 1838 to have lain on the parish boundary with Gussage All Saints, at 014.120. At 054.129 in Cranborne is 'the crossroads known as 'Deadmans' from a legendary belief that a suicide's body was buried there' (*SDNQ* 3p207, 1893). A later source refers to it as 'Deadman's Corner' (so called because of fatal motor accidents that have occurred there)' (Parker 1963 p485), a contemporary revision of ideas. Dead Maids' Close in Holt appears on the Tithe Map for Gussage All Saints in 1841. In 1447 there was a *Dedfolkefurlong* in Charlton Marshall. There was a *Deadman' feld* in Sturminster Marshall in 1593, and this is presumably the close in Green Street called Deadman in 1644 (DRO:D60/T25); Green Street Field lay alongside the Roman road to Badbury at 925.018, on the Spetisbury border. In the adjoining parish of Shapwick, Dead Woman Lane Close appears on the Tithe Map of 1849 (*DP* 89p234, 1967). Deadman's Field in Pamphill (formerly in Wimborne Minster) is shown by the Tithe Map of 1847 to have lain on the parish boundary with Witchampton at 963.042 near the course of the Roman road. The remains of a cross on the boundary beween Afpuddle and Turner's Puddle (first recorded in 1839) is called *The Dead Woman*, and Pope says, 'As to the popular name, there was a tradition that it represents some poor soul hanged at Gallows Hill a mile or two to the east' (*DP* 32 p.1viii,1911). And in 1582 there was a field called *Deadman* in Wyke Regis.

Dead Man at Cranborne gives some support to the theory that all these names commemorate suicide burials, but the usual form of such names from the eighteenth century onwards gives the name of the dead; thus Betty's Grave in Wool and Morgan's Grave in Lyme Regis, and in Somerset Mary Hunt's Grave (Ilminster), Cannard's Grave (Shepton Mallet), and Webber's Grave (Wellington). There is an anonymous Maiden's Grave Gate on the border of Tyneham and Steeple, beside the present road; W. R. G. Bond thought that two pack-horse tracks crossed here (*DP* 58p137, 1936). The name is locally reckoned to mark the burial place of a suicide, and Pennie identifies her as an East Lulworth girl called Jane Gilbert, who hung herself in a barn after her boyfriend left her and went to London; she was buried at the crossroads, with a stake driven through her, and earth heaped up around the stake (Pennie 1827 3p180). However, the majority of Dead Man placenames are not given to crossroads, and forms like the *Dedfolkefurlong* at Charlton are obviously inapplicable to individual suicides.

It is also possible that the 'dead man' names for coppices and fields preserve the memory of murderers' victims. In Holford (Somerset) beside the road that runs over the crest of the Quantocks, is a place called Dead Woman's Ditch where a tinker called Walford hid his wife after killing her, and nearby is Walford's Gibbet where he hanged for the crime, in 1761 (Tongue 1967 p98). This sounds similar to the Affpuddle story, except that the murderer is associated with the grave here as well as with the gallows. The most satisfactory explanation of the names is provided by traditions at a coppice called Kit's Grave at 976.193 on the border of Dorset and Wiltshire at the junction of Sixpenny Handley, Bowerchalke and Ebbesbourne Wake. The story is that a nomadic old woman who frequented those three parishes died at their common border. None of the three churches would take her, so they buried her where she was found (Parker 1963 p482). The belief that she died at the border point is probably the only fictional element here. Significantly, in Surrey two places bear the name Beggars Bush 'in connection with human burials at a thorn tree beside an ancient track along a parish boundary' (*SDNQ* 24p194, 1943). What we have, from the 15th to the 18th century, is a custom of burying at parish boundaries, sometimes beside a road. The people who lie in these unconsecrated graves are the rejected members of the community – suicides, murderers, or foreigners (at Sturminster Newton the north side of the churchyard was 'devoted to the burial of strangers and still born infants' – DRO:MR44p34 – such was the old prejudice against people from outside). It seems beyond dispute that this custom is a survival of the seventh-century practices of pagan burial, for the pagan interments, like their later equivalants, were made on boundaries and often beside a road. Even the geographical distribution matches, for (granted that the placename evidence is biased to eastern Dorset in any case) both the early and late burials come from the area of Cranborne Chase. A gradual change of values has taken place. First there were coexisting pagan and Christian settlements, with different traditions of burial, Then, when Christianity was adopted, it was the outsiders –strangers, and people who by murder or suicide had rejected the Church and society – that received the old rite of heathen burial. It is significant that, in this respect at least, Dorset people have identified themselves with their Christian British ancestors and not their pagan Saxon ones.

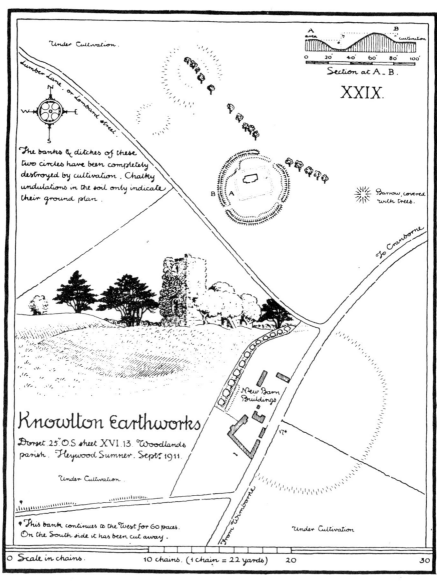

Section at A - B.

XXIX.

Under Cultivation.

Lumber Lane, or Lombard street.

The banks & ditches of these two circles have been completely destroyed by cultivation. Chalky undulations in the soil only indicate their ground plan.

Barrow, covered with trees.

To Cranborne

Knowlton Earthworks

Dorset 25" O.S sheet XVI.13. Woodlands parish. Heywood Sumner. Sept. 1911.

Under Cultivation.

New Barn Buildings

From Cranborne

Under Cultivation

This bank continues to the West for 60 paces. On the South side it has been cut away.

O Scale in chains.   10 chains. (1 chain = 22 yards)   20   30

Knowlton Rings as portrayed by Heywood Sumner in *The Earthworks of Cranborne Chase*, 1913. Today the ivy and elder which shrouded the church have been replaced by neat gravel paths.

CHRISTIANITY

It is often said that the earliest churches were built on pagan sites which had been converted to the new faith. This is a generally accepted belief, and such unlikely colleagues as the editors of *Antiquity* and *The Ley Hunter* have combined in painting a picture of early missionaries arriving at some heathen temple, converting the natives, and erecting a cross or church at the holy place; the basic scenario is varied only by the author's prejudices towards the Christian or the pagan side. It comes as something of a surprise to find that the English churches built on the sites of pre-Christian worship number only three.

One of these is Knowlton in this Inventory. The others are Rudstone in the East Riding, where there is a standing stone, twenty-five feet high, a few yards south-west of the church; and Silchester, where a small Roman shrine lies partly in the graveyard of the Norman church. For the sake of argument, the list can be extended to include some borderline cases where the ancient monuments have not been satisfactorily identified, or where they do not lie within the churchyard. At Stanton Drew in Somerset the church and village lie near the extensive group of stone circles. At Avebury the church lies outside on the bank of the henge. St.Martin's church in Leicester lies on the site of a Roman columnar structure which may or may not have been a temple. (These instances, like most that follow in this section, are taken from Johnson's 1912 study). At Old Yeavering in Northumberland recent excavations identified one structure as a pagan temple converted to Christian use, without hard evidence for either identification (Mediaeval Archaeology 1p148, 1957). The name of Harrow-on-the-Hill in Middlesex preserves the memory of a Saxon shrine, the *gumeningas hearh*, which stood on the hill, and the church of St. Michael on its summit may occupy the site of the earlier structures. This brings the total up to eight. As the number of churches and chapels in England must be something like 10,000, those with evidence (good or bad) for the use of sites of pagan worship will be seen to account for 0.1% of the whole. It is not an impressive figure.

This meagre total has been amplfied by various ingenious arguments. Sarsen boulders and shapeless mounds have been claimed as megaliths and cult sites; traditions of site continuity, themselves the product of antiquarian speculation, have been quoted as if they had evidential value; isolated churches, and churches on hills (for which there are perfectly adequate historical explanations) are cited as if they perpetuated pagan shrines; and confusion is made with other kinds of site refuse which do not involve pagan worship – churches in hillforts, in Roman camps, on Roman villas, and amongst ancient cemeteries. There is no documentary evidence for religious site continuity in England. Bede, who is inevitably cited in this context, only repeats the letter of Pope Gregory to St. Augustine on converting the temples of the idols. This letter, passing between two men both quite ignorant of the English situation, is based on Gregory's problems with derelict temples in Rome, and there is no evidence that its advice was followed in this country. Instead, we read that after Coifi of Northumberland was converted, he desecrated and destroyed his old temple, whose site was still pointed out in later years: no site continuity there (*Historia Ecclesiastica* II. 13).

Knowlton church is unique in that it combines two other categories of site reuse – churches in earthworks, and churches built on pre-Christian cemeteries. The henge around the church survives as the most conspicuous of that group of monuments, while the seventh-century burials around the Great Barrow have been described in the previous section. In order to understand the motivation for this choice of site, it will be necessary to look at other instances of churches in or near earthworks. Of these, Avebury is the only example of a church associated with a henge; otherwise the sites are all hillforts and Roman camps.

15

At Breedon-on-the-Hill (Lincs) the church stands in a hillfort, and excavation has shown that the earliest village settlement was in the fort, around the church. This site deserves a detailed folkloristic study. Its name is compounded of British and English words for 'hill'; sceattas have been found in it; and there is a local variant of the legend of a church which is moved secretly at night from a downhill to an uphill site. At Brownsover (Warks) both church and village lay in a fort on a ridge overlooking river valleys. Danbury in Essex is the 'burh of the Daenningas', and the church stands in this hillfort, though the village has moved. In Buckinghamshire, churches dedicated to St. Lawrence stand in forts at Choles-bury and West Wycombe – presumably Cholesbury derives its name from the monument; West Wycombe has the moved-church legend again. The church of Oldbury-upon-Severn (Glos) lies in the old burh from which, again, the village is named. At Brentor in Devon, St. Michael's church stands on a prominent hill surrounded by Iron Age fortifications, and the name of the hill and parish has been interpreted as Celtic, 'the high tor'. At Caerau in Glamorgan the church lies in a hillfort which must be the eponymous caer of the parish. All these examples point the same way; the earliest settlement lay within the safety of the earthworks, and the church was built to serve it. Later the settlement moves downhill or disappears, but the church remains in the old place. There are two similar developments at known dates. At South Cadbury (Somerset) the hillfort was reoccupied for the second time in the 10th century, when Ethelred II tried to establish a burh there with new fortifications and a mint; the foundations were laid for a cruciform church, but the scheme was abandoned and the church never built. If it had been constructed, its successor would have occupied an otherwise bare hillfort. Similarly at Old Sarum, the hillfort was made the site of a Norman castle and afterwards the cathedral seat was moved there from Sherborne; but when the town was deserted in 1220 the cathedral was demolished.

This interpretation applies to parish churches serving a settlement, but there are also instances of subordinate chapels built within hillforts. In Dorset we have Bindon and Woodbury. Woodbury chapel is first recorded in the 13th century; judging from its site, it would have been visible from the town of Bere in the same way that the surviving chapels at Abbotsbury and Milton Abbas look down on the villages below. Bindon may owe its site to coincidence. The Iron Age earthworks defend the hill behind it in Lulworth, but they are on the other side of a ridge and useless as defence, while the site of the monastery and chapel is comparatively low-lying. It is easily accessible from Lulworth Cove, and this may be the only factor that determined its placing. Elsewhere, St. Blaise's Chapel lay in Blaise Castle near Henbury ('the high burh') in Gloucestershire; in Surrey, the chapel of St. Anne is in a fort near Guildford; at Little Bedwyn (Wilts) a disused chapel, converted into a barn, lies within Chisbury camp; and in Hampshire two chapels dedicated to St. Catherine are sited in hillforts at Winchester and Christchurch. The cult of St. Catherine was particularly associated with high places – she has hilltop chapels at Abbotsbury, Cerne, Milton and Chale as well as the Hampshire instances – so it seems that these chapels are within the hillforts primarily because they are on hills. It is the same kind of coincidence that later led to obelisks and eye-catchers being erected on ancient monuments, and which had earlier induced the builders of Romano-British temples to select sites in hillforts, as at Maiden Castle and Duncliffe in this Inventory, South Cadbury in Somerset, and Lydney Park in Gloucestshire. The coexistence of the chapel and the fair at Woodbury raises the question whether the popular gathering preceded the official construction of a cult building, or vice versa; it is something which can only be decided by excavation. As it happens, there is a modern parallel to this process. The construction of the hilltop cross on Rawlesbury and the establishing of the annual Christian festival here appear to have been virtually contemporary products of the 60s. They are a late example of the hilltop cults which Christianity, like every other religion, has developed as part of its response to landscape.

There is a third category of churches built within fortifications – those which are associated with Roman camps. These form the most numerous of the groups under discussion; there are examples at Bewcastle in Cumberland; Chester-le-Street and Ebchester in Durham; Lincoln Cathedral; Great Castleton and Market Overton in Rutland; Wroxeter in Shropshire; Tasburgh and Caister St. Edmunds in Norfolk; Burgh Castle, Stowlangstoft and Old Minster in Suffolk; Bradwell in Essex; Silchester in Hampshire; Pevensey and Lewes (St. John-sub-Castro) in Sussex; Reculver in Kent; Caerhun in Caernarvonshire; Holyhead in Anglesey; and Llandovery in Carmarthenshire. A glance at the names suggest that twelve of these twenty-one sites lie in villages or manors named after the Roman monument, which suggests that we are dealing with the same process postulated for the hillforts; either there was a lost settlement with the church in the fortifications, or the church was placed there as a nucleus for a community that never materialised. Some of the sites were used for monastic settlements. The church to the north of Burgh Castle (the former Garianonum) survives from a monastry built by St. Fursey; at Bradwell (formerly Othona) the Saxon church was the hermitage of St. Cedd. In both cases the chief motive must have been defence, which would also account for the foundation of the Cistercian abbey of Cupar-Angus in Scotland within a Roman camp; this was in 1164.

Although Knowlton church lies in an earthwork, it is obvious that it does not belong to any of these three groups – it is not on a hillfort, nor in a defensible fortification, nor surrounded by a lost village. It may be where it is because of the proximity of the pagan Saxon cemetery. There are parallels to this from various periods.

Two inhumations, presumably of the Iron Age, were found at the eastern end of the church at Wyre Piddle (Worcs) in the 1880s. The bodies were in a crouched position, facing north-east, and accompanied by iron shield-bosses. At Llanbedr in Caernarvonshire a crouched inhumation surrounded by boar's tusks was found six feet below the level of the churchyard. There are reports of the discovery of urns containing cremations in the churchyards of East Blatchington and Arlington in Sussex but in the absence of any better description it cannot be said whether they were Bronze Age or Romano-British. At Edlesborough in Yorkshire there is a barrow in the churchyard. The church at Brownsover (Warks), which has already been noted as lying in a hillfort, yielded a Roman urn from its churchyard. Another Roman urn was found in the churchyard of St. Helen's, Darley Dale, in Derbyshire (Wilks 1978 p103). At Ludlow the church stood by a barrow which was opened in 1199, when skeletons were found; they appear to have been Romano-British burials. Twenty Romano-British cist burials were found beside the church of Pytchley (Northants) in 1845. Grave-goods were found including a wild boar tusk from a necklace, coins, and a crystal ornament. There was a cemetery of later date, perhaps Saxon, lying nearby, and the modern graveyard was the third in the sequence. At Fimber in the East Riding of Yorkshire the church rests on an oval barrow which had been reused for Romano-British and pagan Saxon interments. Two churches in Kent lie by the sites of pagan Saxon graves: at Faversham part of a skull was found accompanied by a green glass tumbler in 1853, and at Minster another body was found associated with a bell-shaped glass cup. Saxon burials have been found by the church at Mentmore. Taplow in Buckinghamshire, where the churchyard was originally laid out to include a barrow, was excavated in 1883; a pagan Saxon burial with rich gravegoods was found in the barrow.

Returning to Dorset, we find evidence of a greater or lesser kind for Romano-British burials at five churches. A black-burnished urn was found at Maiden Newton. It is illustrated in a sketch of the church by James Thomas Irvine, made about 1850, with the words: 'Vase containing human bones dug up in Court Close; north side of the churchyard' (*SDNQ* 19p156, 1928). At Broadwey, 'whilst digging the grave of the late Mr. Puckett . . . portions of a Roman cinerary urn were discovered' (Hutchins 1861-70 2p490).

In the last century Tyneham churchyard yielded burials 'within a kind of cist formed of slabs of Kimmeridge coal' (Hutchins 1861-70 1p628). I was told in 1983 that the workmen who had shortly before been converting the church to its present use found burials, face down, by or under the porch. These two descriptions, taken together, seem to imply a Romano-British cemetery.

When the walls of Studland church were underpinned in 1881, two layers of burials were found beneath the modern graves. The upper layer consisted of cists made from slabs of the local stone; the lower burials were surrounded by flints and smaller stones. Another cist was found by the north window of the chancel, but left undisturbed. A quern and fragments of a large non-ecclesiastical building had been used in the foundations (*DP* 12p177,1891). When J. B. Calkin investigated the site in 1951, he found that other cists had been found, and was able to excavate one in the northern part of the churchyard. It was of a Romano-British woman in her thirties, whose head had been severed after death (*DP* 74p51, 1952). Another burial was later found nearby (*DP* 77p126, 1955).

'While excavations were in progress [in 1840] for making a vault in Fordington churchyard, immediately underneath the foundation of the north wall were found the remains of a horse with a bit in its mouth, a brass buckle, and other relics of the bridle' (Hutchins 1861-70 2p795). The bit, which is of late Iron Age date, is in the DCM (1846.2.8-10); there must have been a man buried with this horse or chariot. Later, in 1907-8, 'a human skull and horse bones were found' built into the base of a pillar in the south arcade (*DP* 30p166, 1909), perhaps indicating another Iron Age burial with a horse. The extensive Romano-British cemetery at Fordington included the site of the church; graves were found cut in the chalk on a north-south orientation in 1907-8 (*DP* 30p167) and the restoration uncovered a 2nd-century tombstone put up in memory of Carinus, a Roman citizen (RCHM 2iii p574. He is the first Dorset man known by name. Bartelot identified pottery and bone as well as a Roman column in his restoration work (Bartelot 1915 p71) and other surviving relics include bricks, plaster, coins and Samian sherds (RCHM), which could suggest that there was a settlement in the area as well as the cemetery. The earliest phase of the church uncovered by Feacey in 1907-8 seems to be Saxon, since its foundation trenches have a 3:1 proportion of length and breadth suggesting a simple Saxon geomancy. The dedication to St. George is first recorded in 1064.

There is one documentary reference to this reuse of Roman cemeteries, coming from a 14th-century London poet. It is a fable invented about the bishop St. Erkenwald (630-693) and his rebuilding of St. Paul's:

> 'As they dug and delved so deeply into the ground
> 'They found in the floor a wonderfully fashioned tomb,
> 'A sarcophagus curiously carved from Cyclopean stone
> 'All graced in grey marble with gargoyle-like figures'.

The author bases his theme on the idea (taken from Bede) that pagan temples were converted into churches – the sarcophagus contains a righteous pagan whose body has been miraculously preserved – but although the story is probably of his own invention, the idea of the sarcophagus found under a church may have been suggested by a real event.

It is hard to escape the conclusion that the Dorset evidence shows continuity of use at the cemeteries. The memory of pagan Saxon graves may have inspired the Christian building at Knowlton, though as it was a chapel dependent on Horton no further burials took place there. At Studland, Fordington and Tyneham Christian cemeteries succeeded their pagan predecessors, and churches were built where the cemetery lay. This is not strictly speaking a continuity of religious cult, for graveyards were not associated with worship in the ancient world. The presence of burials proves that there had been no temples or shrines.

It is true that at Godmanstone church a Roman altar, dedicated to Jupiter Optimus Maximus, has been found built into the chancel arch (*DP* 86p104, 1964); but this could have come from any Roman site in the Cerne Valley, such as the villa a mile south of the church. Roman altars are not uncommonly found in churches. A list would include Chollerton and Hayden Bridge in Northumberland; Bowes in Yorkshire; Lanchester in Durham; Lund, Halton and Tunstall in Lancashire; Hargrave in Northamptonshire; Tretire and Michaelchurch in Herefordshire; Daglingworth in Gloucestershire; Walbrook (St. Stephen's) in London. Similarly, there is a statue of Jupiter built into the church at Compton Dando (Somerset) and one of Aesculapius at Tockenham (Wilts). Evidently some at least of these appropriations of Roman religious art are intended to represent the triumph of Christianity over paganism, but in no case is it known that the church took over a Roman site. The altar stones seem to have been fetched deliberately from sites in the neighbourhood.

One practice linked to ideas of site continuity is the custom of referring to ancient monuments as *churches*. A field in Wyke Regis was called *camp' de Pokulchurche* in 1460. *Pucela* is a variant of *puca*, so the name means 'goblin's church'. There are instances of prehistoric sites being called the churches of some supernatural being: a haunted round barrow in Longbridge Deverill (Wilts) is Gun's Church; (Grinsell 1976); a standing stone at Minchinhampton in Gloucestershire lay in a field called the Devil's Churchyard (*Archaeologia* 42p242 1869); the site of a Roman basilica at Ickleton in Cambridgeshire is called Sunken Church (Allcroft 1908 p593, giving other instances) and some northern uses of *kirk* at prehistoric sites are discussed in the *Place-Names of Westmorland* 1pxxxi. A Northumberland Maiden Kirk appears in the discussion of Maiden Castle in the Inventory. The earliest reference to the idea is in the 14th century, in *Gawain and the Green Knight*, line 2185. Gawain has ridden in search of the Green Chapel, and is much disappointed when he finds it to be an overgrown long barrow: he exclaims, 'Here myghte about mydnyght/The dele his matynnes telle . . .This is a chapel of meschaunce'.

Two sites which seem to belong to this group occur in the Inventory – Church Barrow and Wild Church Bottom. These appear to owe their names to the open air preaching of Methodists who had selected them for amphitheatres; the chapel at Woodcutts was built in 1853, and that at Verwood in 1850, so the barrow names must belong to the earlier decades of the 19th century. In those years the county was full of men like Daniel Wallis of Osmington who 'took his stand together with others at the Cross Roads, and proclaimed that it was time for all men everywhere to repent' (Simon 1870 p50). 'Considerable groups of listeners' went to hear preachers on the heath at Owermoigne (p55). The closing scene of *The Return of the Native* shows preaching of this sort being delivered at the Rainbarrows.

Site continuity is a more complex subject than has been previously thought. Instead of a simple transfer of places of worship from pagan to Christian use, there have been customs at various times and places of siting churches and chapels on seven kinds of sites – stone monuments, protective hillforts, hilltop landmarks, Roman fortifications, prehistoric burial places, Roman and Saxon cemeteries, and villas. The history of Knowlton has become more complex and fascinating. Out goes the idea of Christian missionaries setting up a church in the henge where (by some remarkable feat of tradition) a memory of religious use had survived for three thousand years; instead the story must have been something like this. Neolithic settlers created a religious landscape based on four henges in the valley of the Allen. The site is respected by their successors who set up burial mounds, including the Great Barrow, in the area. Time passes, and the old cult is forgotten; the land is being worked by Christian Romano-British farmers, two of whom fix the boundary of their estate using the old monuments as landmarks. In the seventh century the smaller, northern farm passes into the hands of a pagan English colonist, who dies and is buried after the custom of his people in a barrow – his son selects the Great Barrow, which lies away from the farm on the estate border, and the site becomes a recognised cemetery. In about 700 Dorset is annexed by the kings of Wessex, who take over the lands to the south of the estate border; the principle farm here lies just under Knoll Hill, so the new occupant calls it and its estate Knowlton.When the county is divided up for church administration, both estates are part of the area served by priests from Horton, where later on (961) a monastery is founded: but the memory of the cemetery at the Rings survives, and when in the 10th or 11th century the monks at Horton are willing to pay for a chapel to serve these outlying areas, the people there request that it be built among the earthworks. And there it remains.

SURVIVALS

The interpretation of modern folklore as a survival of pre-Christian customs and beliefs has now been generally discredited. In a series of studies and monographs, folklorists have shown that traditions need to be interpreted as reflections of the societies which create and elaborate them, not as leftovers from some previous order of things. People have taken pleasure in giving their folklore an archaic and 'pagan' look throughout modern times – Dorset has practices like the Shaftesbury Bezant and the football procession of the Corfe marblers which look like bizarre relics of prehistory, but in fact have been elaborated from quite ordinary mediaeval customs. Examples of genuine survival do exist, however; they are traditions which include elements that are meaningless now but made sense in a context of ancient beliefs, and though few in number they are of great historical interest.

There is, for instance, a widely spread idea that treasures of some kind are hidden in wells. Three instances are given in this inventory – Dungeon Hill, Sturminster Newton Castle, and Woodbury Hill. The same story is told of mediaeval sites. At Chideock Castle 'Mr Weld didn't like anyone to meddle with the Ruins . . . there were all sorts of things there, folks said, such as a golden table where the monks used to sit' (C. V. Goddard's MS notes on Chideock). At Corfe Castle there was a belief, mentioned by Hutchins, that before she surrendered to the Parliament, Lady Bankes threw all her gold down the castle well. 'Tradition says there is a gold table at the bottom of a well' at Court Hill in Ryme Intrinseca, 'but none has been sufficiently curious to attempt to find it' (Dacombe 1935 p11). There is a legend of priceless things of silver 'lying in an old well among the ruins of Sherborne Castle' (DYB 1943 4p32). These traditions of treasures in wells are found also in Somerset; at Hilcombe in Ilminster they say a silver table lies at the bottom of a well in the field called Hilcombe Walls, the site of a great house built in 1690 (SDNQ 25p32, 1947). The same belief applies to other stretches of water, such as quiet pools in rivers. Hookey's Hole at Wick on the lower Stour, where a smuggler of that name met his death by drowning, is said to conceal the hoard of gold that he took to the bottom with him (DYB 1975 6p20). These stories all hinge on the idea that someone once threw golden or silver treasures into the quiet water. The odd thing is that this was indeed a Celtic practice, which became extinct on the spread of Christianity, and was never revived as part of the Church ritual; holy wells continued, of course, but any valuable offerings went into the coffers of the Church and not down into the water. Beautiful things have been found in wells, as at Llyn Cerrig Bach in Anglesey, where Anne Ross would date the deposit to the time of the Roman suppression of the Druids – 'a final desperate invocation of the gods in which metalwork from all parts of Celtic Britain was represented, slave chains and chariots being included in the deposit. The gesture was vain, the gods were silent and the priesthood destroyed' (Ross 1967 p24: see also pp27-33).

A similar survival may be represented by legends of phantom coaches, for these apparitions are often supposed to vanish in streams or pools. The standard legend tells that there was once a coach which ran off the road and disappeared into a pool, and that its phantom repeats the fatal journey. Waring has suggested (*DP* 89p331, 1967) that we are dealing here with the Celtic idea of pools and springs as entrances to the Otherworld, and it is hard to think of any other interpretaion. He notes examples at Winterborne Monkton (a pool by the Dorchester-Weymouth road), Stourton Caundle (a well), Holnest (the river at Hunter's Bridge), Stinsford (Headless William's Pond; there is no ghost in this version) and Hethfelton in East Stoke (the stream called the Holy Water, running from the Holy Well). The phantom coach of the Turbervilles has been seen on Wool Bridge, and Dacombe (p123) gives an example of a pond by Trent Barrow. Another of these stories from Bradford Peverell is given below.

These survivals need to be interpreted in the light of the evidence for holy wells in Celtic Dorset. Three such sites have been excavated; one was at Winterborne Kingston near the Roman road, and yielded evidence of religious ritual including the deposit of a bronze sheet decorated with the figure of a hare, a cult animal (*Antiquaries Journal* 33p74). At Horton the offerings made at an Iron Age or Romano-British well included 140 coins, several unbroken vessels, and metalwork. At Norden in Corfe Castle a holy well, eight foot deep, was elaborately rebuilt and given two Roman altars and a flight of steps leading down to the water; here, too, coins were found (*DP* 94p76, 1972).

It is hard to say whether Celtic tradition has *survived* in the sense being used here, for subsequent cultural levels have also had their own holy wells. The very term (*halegewelle* at such sites as Holwell in Radipole) is probably pagan Saxon, and there is ample evidence too for the Christian consecratation of springs which had no antecedent cult. However, some juxtapositions suggest that modern holy wells are to be found in the neighbourhood of Roman villas. At Fifehead Magdalen 'the meadow immediately north-west of the villa is called Holywell Meadow, and still contains on its brow a strong clear stream of *warm* water. I have found that the flow is received into a stone basin of unknown age, with grooving for a sluice and a hatch for regulating the supply' (*DP* 24p175, 1903). A supernatural tradition appears to attach to the Petrifying Spring near Plumber Manor (Lydlinch), which 'somehow forms a swirl of mud which produces a kind of suction capable of drowning a child' (Knott 1976 p78), and this is close to the villa at Fifehead Neville. And at Cranborne, Wake Smart was able to support the theory of site continuity by fieldwork: 'The Crane stream wends its way through a vale below Cranborne, known as the Tything of Holwell. At the distance of one mile and a half, I have had the knowledge for many years of a spot not generally known, where I have discovered indubitable evidence of Roman building and habitation. In the road-side bank I have traced two distinct lines of red brick tesserae, cubes of about an inch square, in lengths of seven or eight feet. . . This spot is in contiguity with a pond in which rises a never-failing stream of the purest water, which flows into the neighbouring stream' (*Arch. Journal* 44p380, 1887). The spring was subsequently recognised as the eponymous holy well of Holwell, and is now marked by an inscription. Unfortunately Mills produces evidence to derive the name from *hol,* 'hollow', and this less romantic etymology is supported by a cautionary tale from Holwell parish. The name here undoubtedly comes from *hol* (Fägersten s.l.), but for all that they will show you the 'holy well' (*Dorset* 83p30, 1980).

Another curious item of modern folklore, which may be a survival from an earlier state of things, is a preoccupation with ideas about the burial of horses. Iron Age burials of the master with his horse, or horses and chariot, are quite common; we have seen two examples at Fordington. If the rite did not fade out with the Roman occupation, it must have ended at the coming of Christianity. Yet the image of man buried with his horse occurs in folklore of a much more recent date. There is a story from Piddletrenthide. 'An old farmer, George Tom, who lived near the vicarage, used to ride his horse round the farm day in and day out. One day the horse died and he told his men to dig a hole in the field behind his house and bury it.

' "Why bury him with his saddle and bridle on, Guv'nor?" asked Jack Tucker.

' "Because when I die," replied old George, "I'm going to buried beside that horse, so that when the day of judgement comes I can get on his back and ride straight to hell". ' (Pike, Piddle 1980 p119).

It was said, when Thomas Hollis chose his unmarked grave in the fields at Corscombe, that his horse was buried with him. At Cranborne Castle 'the late L. D. G. Tregonwell, esq., interred one of his favourite hunters on the great mound, and raised over its grave a tumulus of chalk, which may be seen many miles round, as the hill commands a very extensive prospect' (Hutchins 1860-71 3p381). There are modern technological equivalents, such as the case of a Dorset biker whose father owned land in the New Forest. When the young man died his companions had him cremated and buried him within the Forest, with his motorbike in the same grave (Information 1985).

The same pattern recurs in other counties. At Beaumont Manor in Hertfordshire, 'one of the early owners . . . put his last shirt on a horse, which, failing to win, was shot by Major Grant and buried at the side of the oak. The groom promptly committed suicide with the same weapon, since when both he and the horse are said to haunt the manor' (Wilks 1978 p26). A cairn opposite a modern megalithic folly by the road from Petersfield to Winchester is 'the tomb of a racehorse with silver shoes' (Jones p121); Marbury Dun, a mare that galloped from London to Cheshire before her death, is said to have been buried wrapped in linen with silver shoes on her feet (Simpson p171). A horse was buried beside his master, a surgeon, in his garden at Downton in Wiltshire, in 1798; there was another instance at Salisbury, In 1866 when Queen Victoria's favourite huntsman died, his best horse was shot. The man was buried at Sunninghill, and the horse's ears laid to rest with him (Johnson 1912 p431). One could look further back in time and think of the mediaeval legends of kings sleeping in mountains – Alderney Edge or the Eildon Hills – which, if the Norse parallels are to be trusted, are based on ideas of barrow burials. Here the knights are often resting each with a horse by his side.

Another possible survival is the motif of headlessness in our ghost stories. The custom of severing the head of a corpse after death and before burial is well-attested in Romano-British Dorset. Such burials have been found at eight sites; at a Dorchester cemetery – a burial with head placed between the knees; Poundbury – a woman with head at the feet; Kimmeridge – an elderly woman, whose head was severed and placed between her legs, while the jaw was cut from the head; Studland – the woman from the churchyard, whose head lay by her left foot; Todber – a woman whose head, with the first three vertebrae, lay by her shins; Woodyates – a burial with the head and first four vertebrae lying by the legs;

and Wor Barrow – two burials with skulls lying by the left leg (These instances are all given in Harmen, Molleson and Price 1981; their numbers for them are 13, 22, 34, 42, 44 50 and 51). More recently a decapitated burial has been found at Fordington Old Vicarage – it was of an old woman whose head, with the first three vertebrae, lay between her knees (*DP* 103p55, 1981). A burial of the 1st century at Herston in Swanage had the jaw removed, as at Kimmeridge (*DP* 96p54, 1974).

Although the best examples are Romano-British (and, elsewhere, pagan Saxon) the practice may have originated earlier. Under the inner rampart of Flowers Barrow was found an extended inhumation, probably of a man, lying with the head to the west; he had evidently been decapitated since the skull rested upright looking back at the body (Pennie 1827 2p85). The custom is hard to interpret. Several of the burials are of relatively high status; the woman at Kimmeridge lay in a cist, and that at Todber in a leaden coffin. Evidently the rite was not disrespectful, even though it is accompanied at several sites by burials face down. The presence of the upper vertebrae shows that the heads were only severed, and not placed on a pole. It is tempting to regard the custom as an extension of the Celtic cult of the head, with decapitation taking place after death so that the deceased could be used as an oracle. Similar, though less gory, is the mediaeval and modern belief that dying people were endowed with an abnormal power of prophecy.

These decapitated burials may shed some light on the problem of headless ghosts. The stock ghost of fiction and cartoons, a transparent Elizabethan gentleman with his head under his arm, is so familiar that we do not regard his headbearing as problematical at all. But why should he be so portrayed? We bury our dead intact: it is curious, at least, that they should return in two pieces. The motif, which goes back to 1473, is not confined to people; it extends, as we shall see, to men, women, dogs, sheep, and horses alike. A headless horse is hard to imagine: I have seen attempted pictures of them, but they fail to horrify. It is obvious that the motif of headlessness is being applied *ad lib.*, without any attempt to imagine its appearance.

There are 27 traditions of headless ghosts in Dorset, and three sightings. Set against a background of some 500 hauntings in the county, these account for about 5% of the total. The 1:9 proportion of sightings against traditions is very large, even compared to traditional types like White Ladies and Black Dogs, while popular modern phenomena like poltergeists may have only one or two traditions recorded, against a dozen observed cases. We may take it that headless ghosts are more talked about than observed.

Phantom coaches with headless occupants or horses occur at Bradford Peverell, Kingston Russell, Loders, Long Crichel, Lytchett Matravers, and Mappowder. A phantom coach with headless occupants rides accompanied by a ghost dog at Shipton Gorge; one disappears into a hole at midnight in Wimborne; one is associated with a murder legend at West Lulworth; and one carries William Doggett, the embezzling stewart and later vampire of Eastbury House, at Tarrant Gunville.

Headless riders run at Lydlinch and Portesham, and at Poyntington, where the group of several men and a woman are associated with a skirmish in the civil war.

Phantom funerals are borne by headless mourners at Lytchett Minster, Milborne St. Andrew, and Powerstock.

Headless black dogs occur at Shipton Gorge and Yetminster.

A headless man occurs in the gardens at Athelhampton; at Portesham, sitting on a gate; there is an unidentified headless figure at Blandford; a headless girl in the churchyard at Kinson; a headless white lady at Shipton Gorge; and a headless woman associated with an historical legend at Pimperne.

Three figures are said to carry their own heads; a headbearing monk who walks from the Manor to the church at Witchampton; St. Juthware's ghost flitting between two gates at Halstock; and Sir Walter Raleigh (the only historically headless member of the group) at Sherborne.

All these traditions, except where otherwise stated, appear on roads or tracks. The same preference appears in two out of the three sightings. In 1907 two men in an unidentified village walking by a pond saw a headless sheep coming towards them and (illogically) bleating. In the morning of 4 July 1976, a Corfe Castle man was driving home when he saw, at the bridge by the Castle, 'a white figure, headless, and seemingly wearing a long nightgown, drift across the road in front of me'. And last year the poltergeist at the Royal Oak in Dorchester manifested itself to a woman spiritualist, in the Ladies' Toilet, as a headless man. It appeared a few weeks later in the cellar as a man in a cape with a tricorn hat and an indistinct swirling face, and continues to shift beer-barrels at the time of writing.

This historical motif of headlessness has not been satisfactorily explained by historical or traditional origins. Some writers have proposed a symbolic interpretation – Theo Brown, for instance, suggests that it represents a dichotomy between intellectual and emotional functions among the story-tellers – but such an interpretation supposes that there was an initial motif which was then symbolically adapted. The headbearing of St. Juthware at Halstock may offer a clue. She was a saint (of doubtful historicity) who was decapitated by her brother after a family misunderstanding, and took her head to church to lay it on the altar. This is fairly common behaviour among saints, such as St. Osyth in Essex or St. Dubritus in Porlock; the earliest case (according to the French hagiologists) was St. Denis of France, who carried his own head after being martyred. When asked how he did it, he said, 'C'est le premier pas qui compte'. The martyrdom of St. Denis was invented in the 8th century.

It is likely that the saint's legend is the origin of the headless ghost; in a case like that of St. Juthware there has been an obvious historical adaption from the image of the saint to the image of the local ghost. The hagiographical legend may simply be a narrative formed to explain the popular image of the saint bearing his or her own head, as a sign of a decapitating martyrdom, but the supernatural aura surrounding the feat suggests a more ancient origin. The evidence, from Dorset and elsewhere, for decapitation as a funeral rite may serve to explain the popularity of headless saints in the Middle Ages, and of headless ghosts in our own times.

GATHERINGS

The use of ancient monuments for popular gatherings shows folklore at its most practical. The tradition of using old sites coincides with the need to select central, easily visible sites for an assembly on neutral ground. The two oldest instances of this tradition are hundredal moots and fairs.

A hundred was a group of estates joined together for administrative and legal purposes, whose principal meetings took place twice a year at an agreed site, the hundredal moot. In 1086 Dorset contained 39 hundreds. 7 were based on church land and 6 on royal manors; of the rest, 15 met at ancient monuments and 11 at other geomantic sites. The hundreds of *Albretesberga*/Cranborne, Bere, Knowlton and Puddletown, which were all based on royal manors, used ancient sites as their moots; this raises the possibility that some of the other six royal hundreds may have done likewise.

The fifteen hundreds meeting at ancient monuments were Badbury at the hillfort; Bere at Hundredsbarrow (later the moot of a separate hundred); Combsditch at some point on that earthwork; Culliford Tree at a barrow; Eggardon at the hillfort; Hasler at a barrow; Knowlton (presumably) at the Rings; *Celeberga*/Loosebarrow at a barrow; Modbury at a barrow of that name in Sydling; Puddletown at a *Motborow*; Rowbarrow/Ailwood at a barrow; and Uggescombe at a *Motbeorh*. There were also *Langeberga* Hundred, which must have met at a long barrow; Hutchins says that the site was Grinsell's Pimperne I, and there seems no reason to doubt this, although other sites have been suggested – Chettle II (by Anderson), Tarrant Rawston I (by Mills) or a barrow on Ashgrove Down in Donhead St Mary, Wilts. (by Watson 1890 p4). *Albretesberga* was virtually coterminous with the later Cranborne Hundred, and by analogy one would expect the barrow to lie near the royal settlement. *Hunesberga* Hundred comprised land west of the Stour at Blandford, but the site of the barrow is unknown.

Why were prehistoric sites chosen as meeting-places? Accessibility must have been the most practical motive. Badbury stands on Roman roads, while Knowlton and the Cattistock barrow are near one. The south Dorset ridgeway runs past the Longbredy barrow, Culliford Tree, and the Hasler site. But if ease of access was the only motive, crossroads would have been a likelier choice. There does not seem to have been any bias towards conspicuous sites: of the nine barrows, all but two (Culliford Tree and Hundred Barrow) have now worn away, which suggests that they were never very conspicuous in the first place, and Hasler barrow named from the hazel scrub around, must have been inconspicuous from the beginning.

Badbury, Culliford Tree, Hundred Barrow and the Longbredy barrow were on parish boundaries: the use of ancient monuments, even small ones, as landmarks is so common that this may have determined their role as meeting-places, standing neutrally on the ground between tithings in the Hundred. Similarly among the other hundreds the stone of Stone, the hill of Sixpenny and the rest seem to have lain on boundaries. This in itself suggests an archaic origin for the moots, since it points back to the sixth and seventh-century use of boundary barrows as the sites of burials; but the documentary evidence unequivocally dates the English hundredal system to the tenth century and no earlier. The obscurity of some of the sites suggests that pre-existing moots were incorporated into the hundredal system. Modbury Hundred must, for instance, have taken its name from a barrow used for some sort of non-hundredal moot. Similarly, Modbury in Swyre (in the Inventory) and the parish of Motcombe bear witness in their names to the existence of unofficial moots.

Two placenames have been thought to record ancient sites used for assemblies. *Cosloe* (1778-88) or Costlows (1819) in Arne (a hillock at 972.881), and *Costlow* (1841) in Holt, are derived by Mills from *Cost* and *hlaew*, 'mound where a trial was held'. This ident-ification is supported by the analogy of Coaselow Wood, *Costelowe* in 1220, in Abney (EPNS Derbs. 1p25): but *hlaew*, though a common enough word in Derbyshire, is absent from Dorset. The only instance, and that a doubtful one, is Winslow (Winsload 1838), perhaps 'Wine's *hlaew*'. Since no trials on a mound are recorded from Arne or Holt (though there are many moot barrows elsewhere in the county), it seems that a new etymology is needed.

The second adaption of ancient sites for assemblies, their use as a base for fairs, is attested from an early date by the finding of coins within them. Sceattas and other coins of the eighth century have been discovered at Walbury in Combe (Hants), Hunsbury in Hardingstone (Northamptonshire), St. Catherine's Hill at Winchester, Old Sarum, and Breedon-on-the-Hill in Leicestershire, all instances suggesting that the earthworks were recognised centres for fairs (Hill and Metcalf 1984. I owe this reference to Laurence Keen).

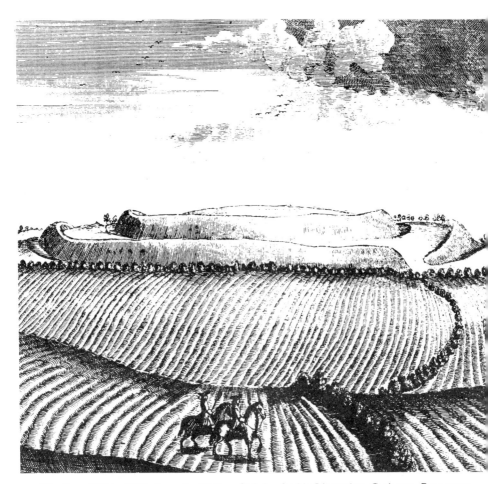

Woodbury Hill in 1724, drawn by William Stukeley for his *Itinerarium Curiosum*. Permanent houses have now been built within the ramparts, and oaks have been planted around them.

In the Inventory there are the coins found in Spetisbury Rings and those which, although recovered from the land below Hod Hill, suggest that the hillfort itself was acting as a focus of some kind. Four Dorset sites are associated with fairs or popular gatherings at a later date: Knowlton, Lambert's Castle, Poundbury and Woodbury. In addition there were the games of 1798 at Maiden Castle, apparently never repeated. The growth and be regarded as immemorially old. At Poundbury there were no popular gatherings before the 18th century, and the fair there only came into existence because of a sanitation act in 1830; yet it seems to have been accepted by most of the fair-goers as an ancient custom. Even Woodbury Hill Fair only goes back to the 13th century. Poundbury and Maumbury, being on the outskirts of Dorchester, naturally attract the attention of anyone wanting to organise a meeting, a play, or a market. In addition to the documentary evidence, there are photographs and sketches showing Maumbury being used as a convenient grandstand for

26

crowds to watch horse-trading, the new railway, H.M. the Queen, and similar attractions.

These gatherings should produce more archaeological evidence than any other kind of folklore, but it does not appear to have been recorded. Woodbury, the richest site, has not been excavated at all, nor has Lambert's Castle. Although the drunken fair-goers at Poundbury and the pressing crowds at Maumbury must have abandoned large numbers of artefacts, they do not seem to have been identified (except vaguely as 'post-mediaeval finds') by the excavations there.

Two places served as the meeting places of gipsies, Culliford Tree and Tinkers Barrow. It is possible that at the former the travellers were perpetuating the older use of the site for moots.

The most recent version of a gathering at the ancient site is the custom of dancing on a May morning on the Trendle (Wessex Morris; since 1978) and Maiden Castle (Portland Royal Manor Morris; since 1985). This is reminiscent of earlier customs, such as the Somerset practice of climbing hills like Dunkery Beacon to watch the sun dance for joy on Easter morning; but it is a purely local development, inspired by a misguided but productive belief in the nonsense about the Cerne maypole.

LANDMARKS

The favourite form of landmark in the county is a beacon; these are set on 25 of Dorset's ancient monuments – Abbotsbury, Badbury, Bind Barrow, Blackdown, Bulbarrow, Chalbury, Eggardon, Hambledon, Hardown, Hod, Maumbury, Melbury Penbury, Pilsdon, Poundbury, Rainbarrows, Seven Ditches, Shipton Hill, Thorncombe, *Toten Berg*, The Verne, Wardstone, Werybarowe, Woodbury, and Wor Barrow. There is one other site for whose beacon there is less satisfactory evidence. At Arne, 'on the top of the hill above the chapel is a barrow, which seems to have been used for a beacon, there being a very extensive prospect' (Hutchins 1774 1p24); but there does not seem to be any confirmation of this.

Most of these beacons were for military use only, but I have discussed them along with folklore, since the military use of the fires during war was often succeeded by their revival as bonfires in peace-time celebrations: at Rainbarrow there are two virtually contemporary descriptions of military and festive use of the same site, and at some places, such as Poundbury, the only fires lit were those for celebrations. It is, in any case, important to have a record of the beacon sites, since the structures used have left traces in the archaeological record which would otherwise be inexplicable. The Henrican and Elizabethan beacon was an iron basket filled with burning peats, suspended from a tall pole which rested on four supporting struts and was ascended by a rough ladder. It would leave a distinctive pattern of five post-holes. The beacons of the Napoleonic scare were more primitive, consisting of tall mounds of furze faggots or wooden billets. When burnt, they must have left an extensive layer of ash, and would produce some very queer radiocarbon dates if they became mixed with prehistoric layers.

A beacon was not necessarily a bonfire. It has been argued by Percy Russell (*Transactions of the Devon Assoc.* 87) that the beacons of the Anglo-Saxon period were look-out posts on which a man was stationed when trouble threatened, and from which he ran down to give warning; some such use is implied by *toten berg* in the Inventory. This theory, if true, would disallow any survival of Roman beacon techniques into a later period. The enclosures claimed as Roman signal stations at Abbotsbury and Eggardon have both been shown in recent years to be pre-Roman, and were not beacons. The word 'ward' (OE *weard*, or a supposed mutated variant *wierde*) appears to have altered in the same way as 'beacon': originally meaning look-out, it had by mediaeval times acquired the sense of guiding fire, for Woodsford Castle was originally 'ward at the fort', a reference to the beacon which is built onto the castle wall and must have guided travellers down from Puddletown Heath. This element appears in the Inventory in Wardstone, Werybarowe, and Wor Barrow; as also at Worbarrow Tout in Tyneham, 'a Cryke in purbyke called Wyrbarow' (1500).

There are three principal sources of information on Dorset beacons. The earliest is the Henrican map, made about 1538, which shows the coastal defenses as they stood in readiness for attacks by the French. Several sites on the Dorset and West Hampshire shore are marked out, each with a stereotyped picture of a pole-and-brazier beacon on an equally stereotyped hill. Unfortunately the geography of the map is somewhat eccentric: the compiler seems to have been taken along the coast from east to west, and to have drawn it as it appeared to him from land, so. that Portland does not extend out to sea but curves along the coast, and the Fleet is much compressed. The best interpretation of the map (of which there is a reliable copy in the Weymouth library) was made by H. T. White in his unpublished work on English Beacons, whose MS is in the Devon Record Office. There is an independent interpretation in Cooksey, and the beacon placenames in Mills clarify some points (see also *SDNQ* 13p14, 1912).

This beacon system was the one in use at the time of the Armada. Although there was a plan for communication of the alarm by border beacons to the adjacent counties, the effect must usually have been panic: such, at least, was William Lambarde's excuse for publishing his beacon map of Kent, to show the people which hill they should turn to. The beacons were watched by two groups of men, one waiting to light the fires, and another on horseback, called hoblers, who rode to communicate the alarm.

The second source is the 1804 map of the resources of Dorset when Napoleon's invasion seemed imminent. This shows, amongst other things, the beacons and signal stations which were to give the alarm. The arrangement was more sophisticated, and one beacon now signalled to another (as in the line of Rainbarrows – Woodbury – Badbury – St. Catherine's Hill) instead of spreading a general alarm.

The third source is a pamphlet published in 1897, 'A Record of Jubilee Bonfires in the United Kingdom', giving details of the hills where bonfires were lit to celebrate Queen Victoria's Jubilee. The list is extensive – there are fifty hill-top fires in Dorset alone – and many of the old beacon sites re-appear as the scenes of festival.

Gallows are recorded from four sites – Eggardon, Gallows Hill, Maiden Castle and Maumbury. The story at Maiden Castle may be an unfounded tradition; it is interesting that the other three sites are on royal land. At Maumbury, we have Stukeley's witness that the gallows was set up between Wren's visit in 1675 and his own observation of them in 1723; they were moved again to a new site on Fordington Down in 1766 (*DP* 88p118, 1966). Eggardon is the first site recorded: the gallows stood in or near the earthwork in 1300.

Three monuments or obelisks on ancient sites appear in the Inventory: Chettle long barrow, the Studland barrow, and Weatherby Castle: perhaps one should also include the tree-clump at Eggardon, a failed landmark. The Hardy Monument on Blackdown was built in an area rich in barrows. This custom of appropriating prehistoric sites to the memorials of the gentry is recorded from elsewhere, the results varying from the sad mess made by a folly in the hillfort at Chun (Cornwall), to the obelisk on a mound in Crislow (Derbyshire) (see *The Reliquary* 5p179, 1899), where the builders not only opened the barrow first, but engraved a reference to the excavation report above the doorway of their new work.

Similarly in 1827 Edmund Morton Pleydell built a wall round the Deverel Barrow (Grinsell's Milborne 14) three years after it had been excavated, and placed a stone in the centre telling of what had been found (Hutchins 1861-70 2p64). These monuments on old earthworks provide an interesting parallel to the site continuity of prehistoric and mediaeval structures.

Some hills with ancient sites on them have become landmarks in popular idiom, without any physical use of the site. Blackdown, Duncliffe and Melbury are used as weather prognosticators, and both Duncliffe and Eggardon serve in their respective areas as typical images of antiquity.

NAMES

Out of the wide variety of names given to ancient monuments in Dorset, three kinds seem to have been conceived out of the images of folklore; these are the names relating to birds, to the size of the monuments, and to their number.

The most popular of birds seem to be the cuckoo. There are eight sites in the county named Cuckoo Pound or Pen. The allusion, as has long been recognised, is to a legend of foolish villagers which circulated by means of chap-books, like that about the Wise Men of Gotham, and became localised at various towns and villages. Wareham is its scene in Dorset: 'It was at Wareham that the cuckoo was first heard in the county and strangers frequenting Wareham Spring Fair, formerly held on April 6th, were wont to confirm this statement, but, says my informant, there came an April fair day when the note of the cuckoo was not to be heard, and it also happened that this season's produce was very late in ripening. The wise men of Wareham decided that the backwardness of the season was to be attributed to the non-arrival of the cuckoo, and they devised a plan whereby the bird should be compelled to become a permanent resident. The following year the cuckoo was both seen and heard at Wareham Fair, and the wise men of the town immediately erected a high fence around the field in which the bird was located. The cuckoo observed this erection with contentment, but when the work had been completed, it flew away. 'Oh!' said one of the wise men of the town, 'we ought to have made our fence a little higher' ' (*DCC* 29 Sept. 1904). The fenced field is not identified, but it may have been the enclosure at the corner of the walls of Wareham known as the Bowling Green; there were fairs held there.

It was a common saying in Purbeck (recorded in Bond 1956 p112) that the cuckoo comes in time for Wareham Fair, to buy himself a pair of breeches. (For the sale of breeches at another fair, see Woodbury in the Inventory). There is a Cuckoo Fair at Towednack (Cornwall), and Heathfield Fair (Sussex) is also known as Cuckoo Day. In Hampshire, on the 15th April, 'the cuckoo goes to Beaulieu Fair to buy him a great coat' *(English Dialect Dictionary* s.v. Cuckoo).

The Cuckoo Pen in Corfe Castle is first mentioned by the 1888 O.S. 'Close to Wytch Farm . . . are the remains of an old circular rampart about 100 feet in diameter. A few trees stand in the rampart itself, and the stumps of others are visible. It is named on the Ordnance Map 'Cuckoo Pen', and by this name it is known by the local inhabitants' (*SDNQ* 17p67, 1921). It lies at 977.856.

The Cuckoo Pound at Langton Matravers, by the parish boundary, also appears on the 1888/9 O.S. 'About a mile south of Leeson . . . is a small plantation of stunted trees surrounded by a dry stone wall. It is of an irregular quadrilateral shape and measures about 70 yards by 80 yards. It is named 'Cuckoo Pound' *(Ibid.)* This is at 008.776.

The fieldname *Goocroft*, 'Cuckoo Croft' (1749) in Arne, may belong to this group. A wood at 867.833 in East Lulworth was a Cuckoo Pound (1888) and a Cuckoo Pound in

Tyneham is located on the estate map in the deconsecrated church there. It lies in a field at 885.803, and is a roughly oval enclosure on a rise in the ground, partly covered by scrub. It can be seen from the adjacent road, or by looking down from Whiteway Hill; unfortunately it is impossible to investigate more closely without being blown up by army debris.

In 1888 there was a plantation called Cuckoo Pound in Bere Regis (at 865.904), and a wood called Cuckoo Pound in Witchampton (at 999.071).

An island in the Frome, now in Bradford Peverell but formerly in Charminster, was called Cuckoo Pond. Alfred Pope, who lived in the parish, wrote 'there is a 'Cuckoo Pound' near Wrackleford . . . described in the Tithe apportionment map or plan for that parish dated 1839, as meadow, containing 1r. 34p. It is an island formed by the river Frome almost circular in shape. When I first knew it, in 1885, it was covered with stunted ash trees, these have now mostly decayed or been removed.This same plot is described in Jennings' Survey. 1807, as 'Cuckoo Plot' meadow, 3r.7p, and is shown with water on three sides only . . .

'I am informed that there is a 'Cuckoo Pen' in the adjoining parish of Frampton, upon which two cottages have been built, but I know nothing of its early history' (*SDNQ* 17p82, 1921).

A study of this placename (Field, 1913) concluded that it was attached to hillforts or to minor earthworks near them; the Dorset instances have therefore been discussed as if they were ancient monuments. However, all the evidence from this county suggests that the name was given to the earthworks round modern tree plantations. From the names of neighbouring, and probably contemporary woods – Botany Bay, Newfoundland Plantation – the Dorset Cuckoo Pens seem to have been so called in the 18th century.

There is also a suprisingly large number of barrows named after birds, principally birds of prey. Even though some of the *beorh* names may in fact be hills, and some of the etymologies are uncertain, the list is still a large one: *beorh* is compounded with *earn*, 'eagle', at *Yon* or *Yarn Barrow* (1777) in Bere Regis and at *Erneborge* (before 1372) in Sixpenny Handley; with 'hawk' at *Hawkesbarrow* in Bere (1776; this is Grinsell's Bere 8, which was used as a boundary mark for the manor's West Field), and at Hakesbury Hill in Canford Magna (1811; perhaps named after Grinsell's Poole 31. The Hill is Lodge Hill in 1887); with 'crow' at Crow Barrow in Winterborne St. Martin (1841); with *ule*, 'owl', at Woolsbarrow (1774) at Bloxworth, and Hulbarrow (1841) in Gussage All Saints; with *corn*, 'crane', at *Cornebarrowe* (1612) in Moreton, and Conebary (1902), perhaps the present Kimber Close, in Puddletown; with *cyta*, 'kite', at Kit Barrow (1838) in Winterborne Houghton; with *hraefn*, 'raven', at Rainbarrows (1878) at Puddletown; and finally with *speht*, 'woodpecker', at Spetisbury. It is remarkable that this last site should be called locally 'the Hill of Yaffies or Green Woodpeckers' (Knott 1976 p175): the name has changed in form but survived in meaning.

Reference to eagles, however unlikely they may appear, are known from other kinds of site. *Aernelei* (1129) in Bincombe is 'wood or clearing frequented by eagles'; at Corscombe there was a lost settlement of *Ernelai*; and *herneshulle* or *Erneshull* (early 13th century) in Gussage all Saints is 'eagles' hill'. The bird in question is probably the white-tailed eagle, still known as the *ern* in some dialects. A Golden Eagle was said to have been caught at Blandford in 1908, but the ornithologists of the DNHAS regard this and other reports of Golden Eagles as mistakes for the white-tailed eagle which is allowed as a rare vagrant. (see *DP* 55p186, 1933; 61p151, 1939). Eagles of some kind, therefore, could have been seen in mediaeval Dorset.

It is hard to interpret these names as ordinary zoological descriptions – 'barrow frequented by eagles' and so on. If this were the case, one would expect bird names to be proportionally rarer than those of animals, and animal names to concentrate on those creatures like the fox, the badger, or the rabbit, which are accustomed (to the dismay of the archaeologist) to burrow into any conspicuous earthwork. This is not the case. Rabbits are represented by Coney's Castle, and foxes by *foxbergh* (1280) at Knowlton and *Fox Barrow* (1777) at Bere: badgers are not, as far as I know, represented at all. This paucity of animals and abundance of birds – in eight cases out of eleven, birds of prey – suggests a meaning for these names outside of zoology.

Whatever their meaning, the names apply to hills as well as barrows. Variants on Kite Hill come from Shillingstone (1838), Affpuddle (1838; at 824.945), Puddletown (1839) and Gussage All Saints (1841).

A similar distribution of names appears in the list of twelve instances of *burh* compounded with birds and animal names given by Smith (1p61, 1956). There are only three animals (squirrel, frog, and mouse), as against nine birds, including the hawk, owl, raven, and crane that appear in Dorset, and also the rook, cock, ousel, and wren. The list is drawn from throughout England. Smith suggests that the names 'probably denote old, abandoned

fortifications infested or haunted by the creature named'. There are Dorset instances at two hillforts – Dogbury in Minterne Magna (941, from 'dog'), and Weatherby Rings (1811, from 'wether').

But why should birds, particularly birds of prey, be supposed to haunt these barrows and earthworks? There is a group of legends in the British Isles which make birds, particularly eagles and ravens, the guardians of hidden treasure, of the sort supposed to lie in barrows. At Guisborough (North Riding) a chest of gold in an underground passage is guarded by a raven which can turn into the Devil. At Alcock's Arbour, a hill or mound in Warwickshire, a famous robber buried his treasure, leaving it in the guard of a demonic cockerel which tears intruders to pieces. Chaw Gully an old mine shaft on Dartmoor, is haunted by a raven and an indescribable monster which make short work of treasure-hunters. These traditions may be the remnants of a more widespread belief about birds and barrows.

Names indicating the size of monuments are usually conceived in the folk idiom. The earliest reference to a King Barrow comes from Alderholt. It is a natural elevation and not a prehistoric site, which appears as *Kynborghe* in 1404, and possibly as *Kingberwe* in a charter of 944. King Hill at Iwerne Minster appears in a 10th century charter. Kingsettle in Motcombe – 'king's seat' – is recorded in 1270. King's Barrow in Portland, which has now been destroyed by quarrying, was a hill and not a tumulus, for two tenants were presented in 1791 for 'suffering their wall to lye down on King's Barrow' (DP 92p246, 1970); this evidently refers to a large down or hill. King Barrow in Studland (1765) is a tumulus (G.?), as is the site of Arne (G.19) which appears as King Barrow in 1774 but King's Barrow on the 1811 O.S. – a small step towards folklore. Culliford Tree is now Kingsbarrow to the neighbourhood. There was a King Rock off the coast of Owermoigne.

Conquer Barrow (1811) in West Stafford, which appears as Conqueror's Barrow in 1848, looks as if it belongs to this group: but the name of Conks Field on the 1841 Dorchester Tithe Map, derived by Mills from a local surname, shows that the barrow is named after a local landowner.

These names have been supposed to refer to a kingly occupant of the tomb, and the finding of rich grave goods in the barrow at Arne has perpetuated the belief. But the name seems to describe the mound rather than its burial: King Barrow at Alderholt is a prominent hill, and the Arne Barrow appears to have been a large one. This sense is suggested by the uses given for 'king' in the OED, where we find king-bolt and king-post, as well as several plant and animal names, from king-apple and king-auk to king-tree and king-vulture. The EDD gives regional evidence for uses like King-cup, clover, fern, and herring. In all these forms the idea is of pre-eminence or importance, so that King Barrow can best be interpreted as 'the largest or most elevated'.

A similar metaphor was applied to roads. The Roman road from Dorchester to Badbury was known as the King Way; it is *Kyngwey* (1426) in Almer and and Kingway (1839) in Zelstone, while King Down (1591) in Pamphill lies at the end of the road. At Woodlands the lane running east into the village from a point south of Knowlton Rings has been Kings Lane or Street since 1394, though it is hard to see why, except that it passes through a royal manor. (See also DP 64p25, 1942).

With a similar metaphor, four sites are named Bull Barrow. There was a large field called Bulbarrow at Bere Regis in 1595 (DCM: Dorset Suits 5p95); Bulbarrow in Woolland (G. 1) is first recorded in 1625 (Hutchins 1774 2p452); there is a Bull Barrow in Holt (1811 – G. 1); and Bulbarrow is the name of 'another large barrow, recently opened in the hamlet of Plush' (Hutchins 1861-70 4p356). Allowing for some confusion of dates, this may be Grinsell's Piddletrenthide 10b. There is also a Bull Hill in Alderholt (*Bulhill* 1618) and a Bullbarrow (1699) lies just over the border in Henstridge (DP 53p145, 1931). Bulbury in Lytchett Minster, which appears to belong to this group, is Burlebey in the earlier forms.

The use of Bul- in plant and animal names suggests that the meaning here is the same as King Barrow. In Standard English there are the bullfinch and the bulrush; among regional forms are bull-buttercup for marsh marigold, bull-daisy for ox-eye daisy, bull-trout for salmon trout, and bull-thrush for missel-thrush; in each case, the word is applied to a variety larger or sturdier than the rest. (Shipp was the first to make this point; Hutchins 1861-61 4p356).

At the other extreme, four Dorset barrow names contain the element 'louse'. Loose-barrow appears in the Inventory. Lush Barrows in Kinson (1881) lay at 065.943. Louse Barrow on the 1839 Tithe Map at Corfe Mullen is a field at 989.974; it may be significant that an adjoining field is called Bonfire Hill. There was a Lowsborough in Dorchester in 1841. Mills gives the meaning as 'louse-infested, or small and insignificant, barrow or hill', and compares a *lusa beorg* of 934 in Wiltshire.

'Louse-infested' makes little sense, if only because the members of a Hundred court would not meet in such a place. The sense 'small barrow' is less illogical, but there are no analogous usages in the OED. The name may mean 'barrow shaped like a louse', i.e. a small humped shape,or, as suggested by the names *Musebergh* in Tarrant Gunville and Musbury over in Devon, both from 'mouse', there may have been some motive for naming sites after vermin.

As usual, the name is applied to hills as well as barrows. *La knap up Lousedone* occurs in 1270 at Puddletown, and there is an Upper and Lower Louse Hill at 611.161 in Castleton (DP 77p147, 1955). Some of these uses may simply refer to unprofitable land. There was a field called Lowsy Bank in 1751 at Poole; another called Lousy Ground in 1840 at Horton; another called *le Louselappe*, 'the louse marsh', in 1435 at Woodlands. It is hard to explain Louse Lane in Spetisbury, on the 1888 OS.

In a county as rich in barrows as Dorset, there will be names referring to the number of barrows in a group. These numbers extend from 2 to 9 as follows:

(2). Two Barrows (1888 OS) in Dorchester. Two Barrow Field on the Wimborne Tithe

Map of 1847 refers to Grinsell Pamphill 1 and 2.

(3). Three Barrows (1888 OS) in Arne.

(4). Four Barrow Hill (1811 OS) in Winterborne St. Martin.

(5). *The Five Barrowes* (1586) in Tyneham, where six barrows were observed by Legg (p122). *The Five Meers* (1765) in Chaldon Herring, which from Hutchins' time onwards have been the Five Marys. The name (from *maere*, 'boundary') invites folklore, but none has been recorded.

(6). *Sixburrowes* (1615) in Dorchester.

(7). The Seven Barrows (1811) in Wareham. *Seven Barrowes* (1798) in Bradford Peverell, where there are in fact something like twelve barrows. Seaborough – *Sevenberge* in 1086 – is from *seofan beorgas*, but no barrows are recorded from the parish.

(9). See Nine-Barrow Down in the Inventory.

Grinsell has argued (1976) that seven and nine are often applied to barrow numbers 'irrespective of the number of barrows in the group'. This trend, which appears clearly on a national level, is less clearly attested by the purely Dorset evidence, in which only Bradford Peverell and Corfe Castle show a marked discrepancy betwen the nominal and the real numbers. It is likely that barrows, being so common in the county, would be accurately and prosaically named.

GHOSTS

The study of apparitions is loaded with preconceptions, most of them centring on questions of ontology; people are insistent for an opinion, one way or the other, on the 'reality' of ghosts. Folklore is not concerned with this issue. The accounts of hauntings and aerial lights in the Inventory include personal testimony as well as oral tradition, since in both cases the stories which are told (the true concern of the folklorist) remain faithful to a set of recurrent motifs. These patterns of narrative are something that can be studied in their own right.

Accounts of hauntings usually comprise two elements, one fixed and apparently objective, the other mutable and subjective. The fixed aspect of the phenomena remains constant over the years, being definable in vague terms as 'mysterious light' or 'phantom army'; the mutable form depends on a symbolically loaded culteral context which is the same for both traditions and sightings. Two of the Dorset cases make this clear. At Maiden Castle and Eggardon, the same tradition of lights hovering above a hillfort is reported in two ways, traditionally as the activity of fairies, and in the modern fashion as a ufo. And at Lulworth and Creech Grange, a phantom army which was seen in 1678 dressed in contemporary costume, had by 1935 moved down the track and become prehistoric savages, reverting the next year to a band of Roman soldiers. The chronology of the other phantom soldiers and armies confirms this view. Contemporary armies were seen in 1661 and 1678; but Roman soldiers have been seen or reported in 1902, 1918, 1935, 1954, 1969, 1973, 1977, 1978, 1982, and 1983. Throughout the 19th century, when ghosts were being recorded as never before, nobody saw a Roman soldier. The conclusion is inevitable: people cannot see Romans until they have learnt about them, and the Roman phantoms must be ascribed to archaeological education, not to place-memory or discarnate spirits. This does not rule out a partly objective existence for these phantoms, but it makes them of no historical use. We will never, despite Carré's experience at the barrow at the golf links, be able to hear the marching-songs of the legions. And likewise the prehistoric rider seen by Dr. Clay owes its particular form to his archaeolgical expertise, although its general existence as a phantom rider is testified to by other witnesses.

Roman soldiers are the most common form of apparition at ancient monuments. They are recorded as individual ghosts from Dudsbury, Hod and Hambledon, Thornecombe Wood, Woodhouse Hill, and the Buckland Ripers turning – there is also a Dark Age warrior at Badbury – while Roman armies may be seen at Kingston Down, Lulworth, Maiden Castle, Maumbury, and on the Dorchester-Sherborne and Dorchester-Weymouth roads, while they may be heard at Badbury and Winterborne Came; other phantom armies occur at Abbotsbury, Badbury, Creech Grange and the Winterbourne Abbas road. There are phantom riders at Bottlebush Down, Ridgeway Hill and Sixpenny Handley; the phantom funeral at Marnhull represents another kind of ghostly procession.

A White Lady walked near the barrow at Ashmore, and a Black Lady was seen among the ramparts at Badbury. With these can be compared the eponymous maidens of Maiden Castle, if these were indeed supernatural beings thought to haunt the site. Fairies in archaic costume were seen at Wilkswood and Wimborne St. Giles. Three supernatural beasts are recorded – the dog at Blackdown, the wildcat at Sturminster Newton, and the raven (fictional in origin) at Badbury. Mediaeval names show that goblins of various kinds haunted the monuments then; there were bugs at Buckbarrow in Ryme and Bugbarrow in Bere, and a puca at *Puckysbarry*; a grima (another kind of goblin) at Grimberry, and a thyrs (a sort of ogre) at *Thursdyche*. The pucas seem to have been spirits of watery places, and may have been shape-shifters like modern boggarts, who tease travellers by misleading them in different disguises. Similarly the shapeless thing at Windmill Barrow obstructed a traveller. There were spirits of some kind haunting Lambert's Castle.

Apparitions of lights were seen at three sites, and in each case the form or explanation is varied; at the burning barrow in Bincombe they appeared as ordinary flames, at Maiden Castle as fairy lights, and at Eggardon as a ufo. The phenomena at the Nine Stones were also associated with ufos.

The sounds heard at ancient monuments range from the incoherent to the oracular. At Ashmore there were vague noises, at Whitcombe barrow an unidentified sound in the air all around; at Bincombe barrow music and Culliford Tree, fairy music; at Winterborne Came, the sound of a Roman army singing; at Eggardon, voices were heard in the mist; and again at Culliford Tree a voice was heard giving advice. The variations on the fixed element of a noise or voice are very distinct here.

Three stories are based on the theme of a car unable to move normally. The apparition at Windmill Barrow, which made a cart come to a halt, may be classed with these, and Dorset stories of witchcraft are full of episodes about wagons supernaturally halted. At Eggardon the close encounter of the second kind involved multiple witnesses and several incidents of car failure; at the Nine Stones and Monkton Hill there were simultaneous unexplained car failures. At Maiden Castle the car was rocked to and fro. These stories, being of actual events, bring us to the borders of ufology and parapsychology; but what is of interest to the folklorist is the symbolic analogy with the old tales of mysteriously halted animals and carts. Elfthrynth's horse, too, was supernaturally halted when she tried to ride to see the remains of St. Edward at Shaftesbury. The reality of the thing changes, but the image remains the same.

DEVELOPMENTS

Folklore is commonly presented as a dwindling inheritance from 'the good old days' of a traditional society. The material collected here should be sufficient to disprove this view, since new folklore is continuously being generated and collected. Oral traditions of the 1980s represent the largest single body of evidence in this Inventory. Folklore is not an ancient unchanging heritage, but an aspect of human behaviour liable to the ordinary mutations of history.

The earliest custom discussed here is that of burial at ancient sites, a practice which ceased after the seventh century; it is obvious, however, that it left traditional associations at a later date, for many of the sites of Saxon burials – Hambledon, Knowlton, Culliford Tree, Maiden Castle – continued to attract folklore on new themes. Closely related to this practice are the hundredal moots, for although the administrative hundreds may not antedate the 10th century, the moots which they used were probably ancient regional places of assembly. Both kinds of use took place on the boundaries of manors or estates, and this implies a very ancient custom of making barrows and hillforts serve as boundary marks. The practice may go back through the Romano-British period to the Iron Age (Cunnington stated that he had found aligned barrows used to delimit land at Poundbury: *DP* 16p48, 1895). Evidently there was a common opinion that ancient sites were special places, to be used as guardians of boundaries, homes for the dead, and places of meeting.

At the same period – around the eighth century, from the evidence of the coins – the custom of using hillforts for trade began. In a broken economy, where towns lacked prestige as trading centres and merchants were accustomed to continual travel, it must have been convenient for annual fairs to be held in some conspicuous earthwork. As is usual with folk custom, the holding of fairs in earthworks continued although different sites were used for the purpose at different times – Woodbury was selected in the 13th century, Poundbury in the 19th. The hill-top fairs coincided with other uses, so that at Woodbury a pilgrimage to the chapel, an administrative use of the site as a hundredal moot, and the fair all coexisted, just as later bakeries, livestock markets and helter-skelters would be combined as a single festival. Maumbury and Poundbury are the typical instances of the versatility of the monuments used for assemblies, for every conceivable gathering (down to the rock concert being proposed for Maumbury at the time of writing) has been held in them.

The earliest evidence for beliefs about ancient sites comes from the mediaeval placenames, and these indicate that, as in the modern period, the majority of people thought of them as the homes of apparitions and supernatural beings. Bugs and pucas and otherworldly maidens had their own earthworks, and in 1639 spirits of an unidentified sort still haunted Lambert's Castle. At the same time traditions of a more historical character were being applied to the sites in a first step towards antiquarian study. The people who called the Bindon earthwork 'the dyke of Julius Caesar' in 1279 must have thought about its age and purpose. Two traditions, at Nine Barrow Down and Wimborne St. Giles, identify barrows as the graves of people slain in battle, and this romantic idea is the same as that embraced by the early archaeologists. The name of Battery Bank implies at least a guess at the original purpose of the monument, although the gory legend of Slaughter Barrow is the work of folk etymology.

While some country people were developing the kind of folk archaeology discussed in the first section here, others were content to ascribe the origin of ancient mounds to giants, who were buried at Melcombe, Swanage and Hambledon, and had coffins at Portland;

Maiden Castle and Spetisbury were both shown as being built by giants. Robin Hood, a larger-than-life figure, had his butts at Verwood. The Devil was responsible for the siting of the Hell Stone and Rempstone; he had a Spoon and Trencher at Shroton, in some mysterious way owned (or was) the Nine Stones, and could be seen riding with the Wild Hunt over Eggardon. These traditions may not have been taken seriously; they fulfill the story-telling itch, just as the tales of golden coffins and other treasures have been passed down without any expectation that the wonderful object would ever be revealed.

The most radical changes in folklore from the 19th century onwards have been the result of a growing unification of society. Folk custom depends on the independence of popular pleasures, while folk belief needs an autonomy of popular ideas, and both these things are always coming under threat. The history of Poundbury in the 19th century, a remarkable story of prejudice, conflict and coercion, showed what issues were at stake. When the elections in the hillfort were accompanied by rioting, the authorities had them moved; when Dorchester's bonfire customs (goaded by attempts at suppression) came to violence, the authorities moved them to the earthworks and established a new, tamer festival. The municipal powers seem to have been forever moving one set of assemblies into Poundbury to free Dorchester of them, and then trying to move another out when it became clear that people were enjoying themselves in too independent a spirit. The rioting is no more, but folk custom at ancient monuments still continues to take form spontaneously despite a culture of organised entertainment. The sudden arrival of May day dancing at Cerne and Maiden Castle is the latest addition to a long series, and everywhere an observant traveller will see flowers offered on stones, shapes of pebbles and twigs laid out, and other traces of private cults.

The development of modern folklore has for the first time been influenced by the availability of written sources on previous traditions. In two cases – Badbury and Cerne – a whole cluster of modern beliefs has grown up, as shown in the Inventory, around fertile mis-interpretations of earlier texts. The resulting folklore has an authentic sound to it, it fulfills a role in the same way as earlier beliefs, and only historical investigation is able to uncover its modern character. The need for oral tradition to find a place in a literate society has led to several changes from earlier patterns of folklore. Legends have disappeared, and no new stories about giants or the Devil seem to be current – evidently the existing combination of orthodox and alternative theories has satisfied the need for origin stories. More productively, geomantic theory has come to coexist with academic archaeology as a view of the past. Archaeologists naturally take a dim view of their alternative rivals, but it is clear that for many people the new mystical view of the past is here to stay. It renews the old image of giants, treasure, prophecy and hidden patterns. The other response to the challenge of the written word has been a new emphasis on the primacy of personal experieince. Most of the material collected in the 1980s was testimony at first or second hand to supernatural experiences, so that evidently this kind of response to ancient sites has taken over from the legendary, story-telling approach. We live in an intensely individual world, in which personal knowledge has come to eclipse tradition as a guide to truth.

INVENTORY OF FOLKLORE AT ANCIENT SITES

Abbotsbury Castle   Hillfort

A beacon at this site appears on the Henrican map, and there was a signal station in the 1804 invasion scare. The monument was 'also used for defence purposes during the 1939-45 war, and during the post-war Atomic War Scare period, as an observation post by the Royal Observer Corps' (Cooksey 1975).

The enclosures at the western corner of the fort was conventionally identified as a Roman military signal station (eg. in Warne 1872 p51) until the excavations by John Beavis in 1975 (*DP* 97p51, 1975) showed it to be pre-Roman.

Ashmore barrow   Round barrow: G. 3e

'There was another barrow, over which the road to Fontmell now runs, by Folly Hanging Gate, near Washer's Pit. In this lonely place, till within living memory, strange sounds were made by creatures in the air called Gappergennies ... Of the nature of these sounds I have not been able to learn anything, except that they could be successfully imitated by human lips. When,perhaps, fifty years ago, a metalled road was made to Fontmell instead of the old cart-track, this barrow, which lay close to the old road and on the line of the new one, was dug up, and the bones it contained buried in the churchyard ... On the down, by the roadside, a cross had always been kept cut, opposite the barrow. This has been neglected since the reinterment; and since then, also, the strange sounds have not been heard'. (Watson 1890 p3, 19).

Watson adds, on the authority of a local informant, that the creatures were 'otherwise called Gabbergammies. The late Mr. Stephen Hall, of the Manor Farm, who had often heard the sounds, thought they were made by badgers'.

The account has been repeated and popularised several times, but there are no sources independent of Watson. The account of the barrow is bound up with another story, of a lady in white who was rescued by a serving-woman when hung up over Washer's Pit; and with the belief in 'a woman in white, who has been seen and felt brushing by them, within the last fifty years, by travellers between Spinney's Pond and Washer's Pit. I have heard it connected with the barrow'. The three narratives seem to have become confused through the proximity of their locations. As the collector remarks, it is curious that all the village's stock of supernatural stories should be placed on the same stretch of road.

Badbury Rings   Hillfort: Shapwick

Badbury, together with the roads round about it, is one of the richest sites for folklore in this Inventory. The associated traditions are partly of spontaneous growth, and have partly clustered around the identification of the site as the Mons Badonicus of Gildas and Nennius, the site of Arthur's greatest victory over the Saxons. This identification was first made by E. Guest, and published posthumously in 1883; the association was made on purely philological grounds (Badbury appears in the Anglo-Saxon Chronicle as *Baddan byrig*), but became a popular Arthurian localisation, at least among Dorset scholars. Although this identification has been supported by Kenneth Jackson in the *Journal for Celtic Studies* (2p152), there are no grounds for preferring Badbury to any of the other proposed sites. The identification of Arthurian placenames is usually an arbitrary matter.

Setting aside the claims of Badonicus, we must derive *Baddan byrig* from a personal name Badda. It has been suggested (chiefly by Ekwall in the *Dictionary of English Placenames*) that this Badda was a legendary hero associated with forts. The name appears at Badby in Northumberland, Baumber in Lincs., and Badbury sites in Berks. and Wilts.; in Poyntington, Badbury occurs as a fieldname in the vicinity of seven or eight barrows (*SDNQ* 1p44, 1888). The name is clearly being applied to hillforts, and can be compared to Maiden Castle, Robin Hood's Butts, and other conventional names for archaeological sites noticed in this Inventory. Apart from a proposed connection with OE *beadu*, 'war', and the similarity to the equally shady Cada of the Cadbury hillforts, we know nothing of the supposed hero. The connection with the Irish war goddess Badb is romantic and untenable.

Badbury occurs as a Hundred name from 1086, and the site featured in a brief dynastic squabble when Edward the Elder camped there, leaving his rebellious uncle Ethelwald in possession of Wimborne; this doubtless inspired the traditions of Camden's time, when Badbury was described as 'a hill . . . where stood a Castle (as they say) formerly the seat of the West-Saxon Kings' (Camden 1695 col. 50). But this matter-of-fact tradition has been eclipsed in our time by the Arthurian stories.

Badbury was formerly the home of a breeding colony of ravens. 'It was in these pine trees that the ravens nested. We were told that they had nested there for hundreds of years, and that legend linked them and their prosperity with the continuance of the house of the Lord of the Manor . . . A raven to us was definitely above the status of an ordinary bird' (*DYB* 1932 p129). This colony had attracted interest a few decades earlier. In 1909 the ornithologist R. Bosworth Smith wrote a description of a boyhood expedition to the monument some twenty years before, in which he had got at a raven's nest; and, expanding on the theme and perhaps remembering that these birds were locally thought lucky, referred to the Cornish belief that it was dangerous to shoot ravens, since King Arthur had returned as one of these birds – a superstition recorded in the 19th century and also found (attributed to the English) in Cervantes' *Don Quixote*. These two references had been brought together in *Notes and Queries*, and, though now supplemented by some Somerset material, remain the chief authorities for the Arthur-as-raven belief. Bosworth Smith, in poetic mood, suggested that Badbury would be an appropriate place to see the kingly bird.

Subsequently, in the popular folklore and guidebook literature, this fancy has been taken up and turned into a genuine tradition: 'The victorious Arthur reappears on the anniversary of the battle every year since those stirring days, in the shape of a raven. He flies about croaking his satisfaction as he surveys the scene of his triumph, then off he flies to reappear the following year' (Collman 1975 p22). The most recent account (*Coaster* 12p5) speaks of 'a black raven ghost', and it seems that the Arthurian image is being assimilated to ghost motifs like the annual visit and the return to old haunts. The king is also supposed to appear as leader of a phantom army: 'They do say that if you'm up to the Rings come midnight, you'll see un' . . Legend maintains that he is still here, that at midnight he and his knights ride round the pre-Roman hillfort in ghostly cavalcade . . . People hereabouts will tell you that, of course, Arthur must have been here at Badbury Rings for some period of his life. After all, was not this the last place in England where wild ravens lived?' (*Dorset Countryside* 2p21, 1968). In another version, the phantom army has reverted to its Roman form. 'Some years ago archaeological students, camping on the summit, were disturbed by the clash of metal, the sound of marching men and shouted military orders in a strange tongue. The camp is reported to have been abandoned in panic and one of the students suffered a nervous breakdown' (Wilks 1978, p66). There seems to be a stray member of this company, an old warrior with a twisted leathery face, gashed with wounds, who creeps up on people after dark, with a preference for scaring courting couples. The last sighting was in the autumn of 1977 (*Coaster* 12p5).

There is also a milder ghost, somewhat out of place amongst this archaic barbarity. The *Dorset Evening Echo* of 19 January 1979 interviewed a woman who had been walking on the site in the afternoon with her husband; he looked back and saw, standing on top of one of the banks, an old lady. 'She wore a long black coat buttoned up the front and finishing in a little stand-up collar. She wore one of those hats like Queen Mary used to wear'. The husband turned round to say that they should help her down the slope, but when he and his wife returned to the area they found no such lady.

These ghosts are interesting in view of the popularity of the Rings among the Blandford and Wimborne people as a centre for day outings, picnics and so on. The warrior ghosts who frighten the modern visitor are in part a projection of historical musings on the fort, comparing its bloody origins with present tameness: the past is scary. The Black Lady, by contrast, is a realistic ghost, since little old ladies are quite common at the site on a warm afternoon.

The Dorset Field Club, visiting in 1889, were told of the tradition that a golden coffin was buried between the Rings and Shapwick village: 'What a prize for the Dorset Museum!' someone said. Treves in 1906 supposed that the coffin was buried in the fort itself, as did Eric Benfield later, but these are probably simplifications of the original printed account. There is a Roman road running from the Rings through Shapwick, besides which there is the site of an army camp, and this may be the site commemorated in the legend. (See N. H. Field's report on Crab Farm in *Britannia* 7p280, 1976).

Badbury beacon is mentioned in the 1588 domestic state papers, as a local muster of foot. It appears on the 1804 map, and fuller details of its use at this date are given in a letter from the Earl of Dorchester to Henry Bankes, then MP for Corfe Castle, 'I have to beg of you that you will give directions for an assemblage of faggots, furze, and other fuel, also of straw, to be packed on the summit of Badbury Rings, so that as the whole may take fire instantly, and the fire be maintained for two hours. The general direction . . . is that this beacon may be fired whenever the beacon off St. Catherine's [Christchurch] is fired to the eastward, or whenever the beacons on Lytchett Heath or Woodbury Hill are fired to the westward' (Bankes 1853).

The popularity of Badbury for excursions has led to a rapid increase in beliefs about the avenue of trees planted on either side of the road from Wimborne. In fact these were planted by William John Bankes of Kingston Lacy in 1835. When surveyed in 1973, there were 374 trees to the north and 364 to the south, with 18 gaps which have subsequently been replaced.

The essential tradition is that there is a tree for every day of the year, although in fact there are too many to the north, and probably the south, for this to work. A more perceptive variant says that there are 365 on one side, 366 (for a leap year) on the other. They are variously supposed to have been planted by prisoners of war; as a memorial to soldiers who fell at Waterloo; to mark the death of a farmer's son in World War I; and to record the one year of happiness which Bankes enjoyed with his wife before she died. One informant was certain that they concealed a cache of sovereigns: 'Ther'm yeller boys unner 'em' (*Dorset Countryside* 2viii p33, 1977; *Dorset* 100p32, 1982). Such beliefs are part of an interest in trees as landmarks, developed in response to the local tourism of the last few decades.

Battery Banks   Entrenchment: East Stoke

The name first appears on the OS of 1888, and suggests a tradition of a battle in which the earthworks – which are undated, but usually accepted as prehistoric – were used to support cannon; the belief may have been suggested by their appearance, or may record a reoccupation of the site in the Civil War such as happened at Maumbury.

Bincombe: the burning barrow   Round barrow: G.11

An informant told me in 1984 that one night a few years before she had been riding pillion on a motorbike past this barrow, going up along the road from Ridgeway, and had seen fire on the mound. There was an orange glow around the top, and flames were shooting up from it: both she and the rider of the bike saw this. She felt strongly that the place was sinister, and was unwilling to stop and examine closer. This experience closely resembles the Norse legends (about which the informant knew nothing) of fires which dance around the summit of barrows containing treasure, and which are associated with the evil dead. (The best account is in the *Hervorsaga*. See also a correspondence on 'Ghostly Lights' in *Folk-lore* vols 5 and 6, 1894-5).

Bincombe: the music barrow   Round barrow: G. 5 or 5a

'On Bincombe Down, there is 'the music barrow', of which the rustics say that if the ears be laid close on the apex at mid-day, the sweetest melody will be heard within' (Warne 1866 p1).

Traditions about fairy singing underground are quite common in other counties. At Willy Howe in Yorkshire, 'the peasantry assure you that if any one run nine times round the tumulus without stopping, and then put his ear against it, he will distinctly hear the fairies dancing and singing in the interior' (Wright 1861 1p35). The tradition applies to other kinds of site, such as the maze at Asenby (Lincs.), where there were in 1912 'persons still alive who will tell one that they have trodden it on many a summer's evening, and, kneeling down at the centre,, have listened 'to hear the fairies singing'. They still call the site The 'Fairies' Hill' ' (Allcroft 1908 p602). Both these instances rely on physical exhaustion to bring about the supernatural effect. In Somerset 'the most beautiful music' was to be heard from the large tumulus on Wick Moor, in Stogursey (Major 1913 p108). Fairy singing is reported from a chambered cairn at Strath in Skye, the Broch of Houlland and Trowie Knowe in Shetland, and Mingulay Dun in Barra (Grinsell 1976). A belief in fairies singing underground is implied by a story of sharp practice from Cheshire, where a horse-thief 'lay flat in the road as a rider drew near because, so he said, he could hear 'ground-fairies' singing; the rider dismounted and lay down – and when he got up, the thief was galloping off on his horse' (Simpson p50, 1979).

Blind Barrow   Round Barrow (or natural; mound): G. 2
                    Burton Bradstock

During Burton's celebrations of the 1887 Jubilee, 'the beacon on top of Bind Barrow was lit and rockets sent up' (Gale 1983 p124).

Bindon   Entrenchment: West Lulworth

This monument was known as 'the dyke of Julius Caesar' in 1279. This is a remarkable reference. There are several sites called Caesar's Camp – at Aldershot, Sandy,

Easthampstead, Wimbledon, and Folkestone – but their names have been attributed to the Elizabethan antiquarianism of Camden and his generation. This mediaeval form of the name suggests an unexpected interest in British prehistory, probably derived at second hand through the 12th century antiquarians, such as William of Malmesbury or even Geoffrey of Monmouth. It is curious that in the years 1905-14 the name 'Caesar's Camp' was still being applied to Bindon Hill or Flowers Barrow (*DYB* 1950-1 p183) and that the twentieth-century phantom army traditions should locate Roman soldiers here too.

The abbey of Little Bindon, afterwards transferred to Bindon near Wool, was first built here, and the Early English chapel described by Hutchins and marked on the OS belonged to this community. The size of the entrenchment makes it hard to decide whether the abbey was built behind it on purpose, or merely as an accidental use of a promontory on the coast.

Blackdown barrows   Round barrows: G. 2a-5 Portesham

The domestic state papers of May 1588 describe beacons at Ridgeway and Blackdown, the Ridgeway site apparently lying to the east on the way to Sutton Poyntz. The Blackdown beacon was probably lit on one of the barrows here. The site was reused in 1804; Joseph Hardy of Portesham was responsible for 'setting up and erecting the said Beacon', and paying a local man, William Boyt, 9 shillings weekly over 8 weeks for watching the beacon (DRO: D188B/Z5).

According to an informant in 1983, there is a dog that appears up here by the Hardy Monument, but to see it is an omen of illness or death.

Bloxworth Down barrows   Round barrows: G. 1-12

'There are some burial mounds in a field by the road from Bere Regis to Wimborne. It is said that there is treasure buried in these mounds' (Palmer 1973 p149). The legend may have been initiated by the barrow-digging of Shipp and Durden here in 1854.

Buckbarrow   ?Barrow: Ryme Intrinseca

'Barrow haunted by a *bug* or goblin'. A field called Buckbarrow is the subject of a grant of 1629 (Hutchins 1861-70 4p493). In 1779 two closes called Bugbear, of five and three acres, were part of Ivorhill tenement; in 1808 and 1847 they were known as Bagbarrow and listed in the Court Roll (DRO: D15A/T36).

Bugbarrow   Round Barrow: G. 25 Bere Regis

The 'fielde called Buckbarrowe' is first mentioned in 1617 (DRO: Photo 2&8/11-12), and must likewise mean 'barrow haunted by a *bug* or goblin'. In 1774 it had become a hamlet of three houses – 'Bugbarrow adjoins to the North of Bere' (Hutchins 1774 1p93). The site was recorded as Bug Barrows by M. E. Cunningham, but may be a natural mound (Grinsell 1959).

Bulbarrow   Round barrow: G. 1: Woolland

This is 'the barrow called Bulbarrow, where there was formerly a beacon, at which, 1625, the hundred of Redlane, Brownshull, Sturminster Newton and Buckland were obliged to find watchmen' (Hutchins 1774 2p452).

Bulbury   Hillfort: Lytchett Minster

In 1881 an Iron Age smith's hoard was found within the earthworks of this fort, and Edward Cunnington investigated the discovery. 'I paid a visit to the old woman who was reported to possess several of the objects. On inquiring of her for them, she told me that she 'hadn't a' got 'em'. On my asking what had become of them, she said 'Well, there! I was obliged to send 'em to my poor boy, for he was terrible bad, and did sort o' pine for 'em; and a' thought if a' could have thic there little dog, and nail un up over the door, a' would be better'. I then went to the son's house, where I duly found the animal nailed over the door' (*Archaeologia* 48p3). The 'little dog' was one of the two bronze bulls now in the Dorset County Museum, accessioned as 1884. 9. 114.

Cerne Giant and Trendle   Hill-figure and enclosure: Cerne Abbas

The study of hill figures is unlike any other field of archaeology. Excavation is impossible and the other ways of recovering the date and original appearance of a monument are either unsuccessful or controversial. In the absence of stronger proofs, we have to rely on arguments from probability, based on the style or location of the figures, which offer the best approximation to the truth: and folklore has been used as a support for such arguments. The Cerne Giant, and the Trendle earthwork associated with him, feature in various superstitions about fertility, which have suggested an early date to researchers of varying degrees of orthodoxy and acuteness.

The first reference occurs in 1888, mentioning only the remarkable 'Phallic superstition ... counterparts of which are found in Brittany and India' (*Folk-Lore Journal* 6p115, 1893). This is expanded on by Udal, five years later: 'It is said to be a perfect cure for barrenness in women if they sit on the actual figure of the giant ... but some say that the married couple must actually consummate the marriage on the spot' (*DP* 14p194, 1888). The Breton and Indian parallels referred to doubtless involved sitting in contact with some sacred monument: thus the Breton bride would sit on the Grey Mare in Finistére, and Indian women, in one instance, sat astraddle on a derelict Dutch East India Cannon as a fertility charm. Udal's statement has been repeated by several authors over the last century, including perceptive figures like Harvey Darton, but it is unsure whether any of these references have been freshly gathered from folk tradition. There are recent statements, however, of the Giant's power. 'One hears stories of girls entreating the aid of the Giant', wrote F. C. Warren in 1944 (DYB p68). 'It is quite impossible to live in the district and be aware that not only young girls who fear to lose their boyfriends are in the habit of visiting the figure and perambulating his frame, perhaps with a giggle and hand-in-hand with a girl friend, but grown women as well who fear to lose their mates. Women about to get married, too, as has been told personally by their husbands in later life, used to look on it not only as a normal and respectable act, but the duty of common sense to visit the Giant to express their hopes during the week prior to marriage. Some of my friends tell me also that women of their acquaintance confess to having sat on the appropriate portions of the erstwhile god to assure themselves of the future' (Dewar 1968 p6). 'Several friends of mine have provided supporting evidence for the legend that sleeping within sight of the giant is a powerful fertility spell for women' (Wightman 1977 p98). And bringing the story up to date, the *Dorset Evening Echo* (28 April 1982) tells us that 'an annual pilgrimage to the Cerne Abbas Giant is soon to be made by the Marquis of Bath, his wife Virginia and his daughter Silvy ... Some 22 years ago the Marquis is said to have called upon its power after five

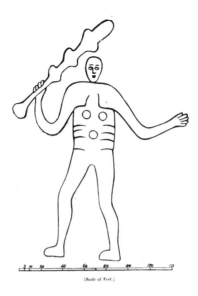

[Scale of Feet.]

The Cerne Giant, in the respectable version presented to the public of 1841 by John Sydenham in *Baal Durotrigensis.*

years of childless marriage. His daughter arrived nine months later, and every year since, the trio visit the Giant where, it is claimed, they talk to it at length about their problems'. The old god does not like to be taken flippantly. One informant in 1984, going out to Cerne for the day with a couple of friends, had had a bit of a giggle playing around on the figure. As the month wore on she seemed a bit subdued, and I asked if anything had happened; no, she said, something *hadn't* happened – not for two weeks now. But everything was all-right in the end.

The early traditions should be taken with a pinch of salt. The bare slopes of Giant Hill – exposed to the elements, and still more exposed to the gaze of bystanders – would make an uncomfortable background on which to consummate a marriage, although the Giant may have been touched or sat on by individual women. The modern customs have doubtless developed from a general interest in the figure and the repeated citations of Udal. It is interesting that a Dorset newspaper of 1850 described a similar belief attached to St. Augustine's Well in the village below. 'We should recommend all lady travellers passing through to rest awhile and pay a visit to the same and they will experience (as the legend says) the ... happiness of having their wish granted within a year' (*DYB* 1923 p78): in plain English, would have become pregnant. Fertilising wells are common enough – Henrietta Maria conceived after a visit to the Queen's bath at Bath, putting her trust equally in science and superstition – and it is possible that the fertility legend belonged originally to the well, and was attracted to the Giant later on. A belief like this can grow up easily enough, as for instance it has around the funeral monument of Victor Noir, a radical journalist under Louis Napoleon, who lies buried in the Père Lachaise cemetery in Paris. 'The private parts under the bronze zip were so exaggerated by the sculptor that Noir became a place of pilgrimage. Young wives, anxious to conceive, touch the bulge and say a prayer. So many have done it over the years that Noir's manliness is being reduced to normal proportions' (*Observer Colour Supplement* 6 Mar. 1983 p29).

The oldest tradition about the Giant is that recorded by Gough. 'There was once observed, in the possession of a pauper in the neighbourhood (since dead), an old thick folio volume, in the black letter, containing accounts of many antiquities of the kingdom, and embellished with impressions of coins from engravings on wood; in which book was an account of the abbey of Cerne and the giant; and in it was asserted that queen Emma in exile found an asylum in the abbey, and that the giant was cut in the hill at the dissolution of the monastery, in derision of the abbot. That the indecent appearance of the figure was expressive of his lust; the uplifted club, of his meditated revenge; and the position of his feet, the necessity of his quitting the place' (Hutchins 1796-1814 3p322). Black letters became obsolete for most books except Bibles around 1600, so that this evidence, if we are to take it on face value, disproves the supposition that the Giant was cut by Lord Holles or his steward during his residence in the village between 1654 and 1663.

'There is a tradition, that a giant who formerly did mischief, having made an excursion into the adjacent Vale at Blackmore and devoured several sheep, lay down on the side of a hill to repose himself and digest his breakfast. Falling asleep, the people rivetted him down and killed him and then cut his figure in the solid chalk. Fabulous as this story is, it is perhaps a proof of the great antiquity of this figure'. (Hutchins 1774 2p292). There are modern variants on the tale. 'They will tell you, half creduously, half to see what you will swallow, that he was long ago caught sheep-stealing, and that the tree-clumps along the road from Dorchester mark his footprints as he went to rest, surfeited, on the hill, where the natives pinned him down and killed him; and the little earthwork above him is the print of his frying-pan' (Darton 1935 p80). Again, 'It is said that a giant threatened Cerne and went to sleep on the hillside. A shepherd boy went up in the night and slew him, whereupon the people of Cerne carved round the outline of the body' (Wightman 1977 p98). The variant forms of this tale show how it has remained alive in the oral tradition.

There are some minor traditions about the figure. 'One of the local legends is that the Giant devoured virgins' (*DP* 22p101, 1901). 'He has come down to the stream to drink at night' (Darton 1935 p80), or 'come down to drink at the Mill stream, when he heard the church clock strike twelve' (Jones 1952 p49). And, most tersely, 'I was told, in Cerne, that he was there to frighten Sydling folk' (Waring 1977 p46). The belief about his descending to drink is told with joke emphasis on 'when he *hears* the clock', for turf and chalk cannot hear. The same belief, with the same catchword, is applied to half-a-dozen heraldic statues on the gates of Dorset manor houses, and to the Langton Herring roadside cross. The Giant is the only prehistoric monument to which it is given, although it occurs at several standing stones in other counties. Recent research, however, has shown that these legends of drinking stones are a variant of a much larger group about drinking statues, and not a relic of some faith in menhirs.

There is another tradition in which the Giant is presented as a supporter of the old Dorset sport of cudgel-playing. Richard Cutler could remember the days at the beginning of the 19th century when Revels Inn at Middlemarsh was the great centre for the savage game; local families – most notably the Shitlers – took on all comers at yearly matches. A man would hold his cudgel in one hand, and have the other braced with padding. He signalled

his willingness to fight by throwing his hat onto the raised platform that served as a ring. The 'stickler' – a word we only use metaphorically today – was the man who saw fair play between the fighters. Cutler says, 'There is an ancient rhyme still ringing in my ears –
'Fi-Fo-Fum
I sniff the blood of an Englishman',
which my nurse told me was the voice of the giant on Cerne Hill, when he heard that the Shitlers had challenged the Somerset and Wiltshire players to a trial-bout on the stage at Revels; that the giant heard of the intended contest, and strode down into the valley to be stickler between the doughty combatants. He came with his club in his hand, and rapped with it on the ground as a signal that the play should begin. Dorset and Somerset set to in earnest, and very soon a head was broken, and the crowd around the stage gave the usual shout – 'Blood, blood, blood!' as the purple stream trickled down from the scalp of the unlucky player. Another hat is hurled without delay on the stage, and other brawny arms are padded for a fresh bout, the new man having his own cudgels, weapons that he had yielded before with success, and with which perhaps he now broke the head of the first victor; and so the play went on with alternative victory, till it came to Shitler's turn, a left-handed player who usually won the prize, partly from superior skill, and partly from the circumstance that his opponents were not on their guard for left-handed blows. These sanguinary revels were genial pastime to the giant. But sometimes (as the legend runs) he would extend his walk and stride over to the opposite hill, where Belchalwell nestles under Bulbarrow, and stretch himself out like a lazy shepherd on a summer's evening, and watch the golden light of the setting sun, claiming this district as part of his own domains, because they bear his own name. I have no idea where my nurse picked up her giant lore' (Cutler 1865 p65). Perhaps she made them up to amuse a curious child; but they have a traditional sound. Like Hutchins's tale, this account represents the Giant as wandering between Cerne and the Blackmore Vale; and seven centuries before, if we interpret Geoffrey of Monmouth rightly, the people of Plymouth had also told a story associating the hill-figure of a giant with a club, lying on Plymouth Hoe, with the local sport – in this case wrestling.

The traditions about the Trendle have been connected with the Giant in folklore theories, though not in actual practice. Colley March, who did fieldwork on both monuments in 1897, wrote: 'Childs, the former sexton, well remembers the maypole. It used to be set up in the ring just above the giant. It was made from a fir-bole and renewed every year. It was raised in the night. It was decorated with garlands etc. The villagers went up the hill and danced round the maypole on May 1. Nothing of the sort is now done' (*Folklore* 10p478 1899). March also refers to the town maypole taken down by the churchwardens in 1635, but this has no link with prehistory. His informant Childs is the only authority for this tradition of a maypole in the Trendle, and his evidence has been doubted by two independent sources. 'That sexton is not accepted as a trustworthy witness by those inhabitants who remember him; and two credible persons still living assert bluntly that the Frying Pan is nothing but the remains of a small tree-plantation, such as many hill-tops bear. The trees died long ago. These witnesses remember the fragments of roots, and both their fathers had told them of the trees themselves'. The informants said positively 'that the Maypole dance was always held in the village itself, in Abbey Street, on the green by the Town Pond' (Darton 1935 p21). 'In regard to the earthworks above the Giant, Mr. Dominy says that 'in his father's time it was made for a fir plantation, the roots of the old trees still being visible'. He also thinks that the Maypole was never set up on the hill but in the village' (*DP* 46 p.xxxii, 1925).

The belief that the Maypole was set up on top of Giant Hill is contradicted both by local tradition and common sense. Although the Trendle was not, as Darton suggests, actually made as a plantation earthwork, it was certainly adapted as such. Sydenham (1841 p46) describes it as an earthwork 'of a somewhat oblong form . . . it is about 100 feet in its longest diameter, has a low vallum, slightly exterior fosse, and a slightly elevated mound in the centre'. Today, as appears on aerial photographs of Giant Hill, the Trendle is a small square bank, with a ditch around it, contained by a larger, more irregular, and lower bank surrounded by a slighter ditch. Evidently the outer bank is the original monument, and the inner one was built to shelter the abortive plantation of firs. This must have been done at some time later in the 19th century, but before the property was acquired by Pitt-Rivers. Moreover, although this leaves the possibility that a maypole was put up in the ring before the plantation was established, such a view is confuted by common sense. A maypole could be anything up to 100 ft. tall; to carry such a weight up the steep, clayey sides of Giant Hill (let alone by night), to renew it every year, and to fit a population of 1000 people into a small earthwork on a steep hill is difficult enough; but to do this without leaving a gaping hole where the maypole had stood (instead of 'a slightly elevated mound') is impossible. I think we can leave the maypole where it belongs, by the Town Pond, and dismiss the sexton Childs as a successful hoaxer.

As fate would have it, though, the spurious account of May Day festivities on the hill has now given rise to a genuine popular practice. In 1978 the Wessex Morris Men climbed Giant Hill and danced in the Trendle at dawn (7.30am), under the impression that they were renewing the ancient custom. They brought with them a replica of the Melbury Osmond Ooser made by a Weymouth man in 1973; after the hilltop dance they processed through the village. The ceremony has been repeated each year since on May 1st, although the Ooser (which weighs a couple of hundredweight) no longer ascends the hill. The audience for a chilly dawn ritual is small; a couple of dozen people turned up for the first dance in 1978, when May 1st coincided with the Bank Holiday Monday, but in 1985 there were only two bystanders.

Chalbury   Hillfort: Bincombe

A bonfire was lit on this hill for the 1897 Jubilee.

Chettle Long Barrow   Long barrow: G. 11

This is one of the sites identified as the meeting-place of *Langeberge* Hundred. Shortly before 1767, that part of the barrow lying within the grounds of Eastbury House was opened by Bubb Doddington, Baron Melcombe 'and a grotto made in the hollow. We were were told that when it was opened a number of Bones were found' but as at Ashmore, these were reinterred. The grotto was large enough to shelter a gamekeeper in a storm a few years later (*DP* 21p144; Hutchins 1861-70 3p567).

Church Barrow   Roman amphitheatre: G. Handley 6.
                                                          Sixpenny Handley

The site (identified as an amphitheatre by Pitt-Rivers 1p24) was 'vulgarly called Church Barrow' in 1865, according to J. H. Austen (*Archaeological Journal* 14p107). Pitt-Rivers supposed that 'it may have been used for Divine worship as early as Saxon times', while Austen favoured the theory that Protestants met here at the time of the Marian persecution, favouring a spot near the Wiltshire boundary so that they could easily escape to the separate jurisdiction of another county. Both dates are probably too early; the 1887 OS shows a Wesleyan Methodist Chapel at Woodcutts, a short way south-east of the site, and the amphitheatre is likely to have been the original Wesleyan preaching ground.

It should be noted that there are two Dorset sites which have the same name, but no folklore. Winterbourne Steepleton 3 and 4 are called Church Barrows on the 1811 OS, and a cottage called Church Barrow (from a lost barrow or hill) stood in Piddlehinton in 1870. In both cases the name comes from their lying near the village church.

Combs Ditch   Entrenchment: Various parishes

The meeting place of a hundred which appears as *Concresdic* in 1086. The bank divides the hundreds of Combsditch, Bere and Loosebarrow in a somewhat confused fashion. When first recorded in 942, as *cinninces dich* (*DP* 55p241, 1933), it served to divide manors and so was probably already a hundredal boundary.

Coney's Castle   Hillfort: Whitchurch Canonicorum

'Conig or King's Castle, as its name implies, is said to have been the headquarters of King Egbert when he fought his brave, but losing battle against the Danes on Charmouth beach in 833' (Turner 1947). The same romantic etymology has ocurred to other authors, with similar developments: in fact the name means what it says, rabbits' castle'.

Culliford Tree   Round barrow: Whitcombe

Still known as such by archaeologists, although Kingsbarrow is the local name now (1982) in use. 'Here the hundred courts were formerly held' (Hutchins 1774 1p419). The name first appears as *Cuferdestroue* in 1086. The etymology is open to debate: Culliford has been derived from an otherwise unknown name *Cylferth*, a contraction of *Cytleferth*, a name which is unknown but is paralleled by two Scandinavian forms, also otherwise unknown. Alternatively, it could come from a word *cylfe-weard*, 'guardian of the mace', used to describe a functionary at the Hundred court: this word is otherwise unknown (Mills 1p196). There may be some connection with the Dorset surname Culliford; a *Galfridus Culeford* of Bryantspuddle is recorded in the 1327 Lay Subsidy Role. The tithing of Cripton owed suit to the hundredal court 'by the service of bringing up to the down (where the court leet is held under a large barrow) a half bushel as a desk for the steward to write on' (Hutchins 1796-1814 2p130), and according to Warne (1866 p5) the court was still being held there in his own time. If these statements by Gough and Warne are to be taken at face value, the open-air moot here had survived or been revived in the 19th century; this would make it the last of the hundredal moots to be held in the traditional way.

The Bincombe tradition of music being heard from the barrow was also current at this site (Warne 1866 p1). A modern instance of this phenomenon is described by H. S. L. Dewar, who tells how a friend 'some years ago wished to purchase a plot of land closely adjacent to the musical barrow. On two occasions she visited the spot, which is far from human habitation, to make up her mind about building a house there. She states firmly that on both visits she heard the voice of an invisible speaker who warned her to desist from her plan. After the second occasion she told her agent she had changed her mind'. He assures us of the reliability of this informant, and adds 'since her visit was not known in advance to any but herself, nobody could have been hiding behind the Culliford Trees' (Dewar 1977).

There was a traditional gypsy camping ground by the barrow; 'so constant has been their use of the tree that one of their queens lies buried at Broadmayne, and for nearly a week, it is said, this hill was a kind of hive of gypsies from all parts' (Darton 1935 p131).

The Devil's Spoon and Trencher   Earthwork: Iwerne Courtney

The name of an earthwork at 887.133. Its date is uncertain, but it is so named in an estate map of 1767, and is accepted by the OS as ancient (*DP* 64p75, 1942).

Dudsbury   Hillfort: Hampreston

'Between Throop and Dudsbury, Riddles Ford (near Redhill Common) is said to be haunted by Roman soldier ghosts and one of these is reputedly the phantom resident of Dudsbury Camp. Local residents whose properties back onto these prehistoric earthworks have seen this lost Roman wandering across gardens as if seeking a final resting place' (*Coaster* magazine 12p5, 1982).

Duncliffe Hill   Romano-British temple and entrenchment: Motcombe/East Stour/Stour Provost

The Romano-British temple here, implied by the recent discovery of votive offerings (*DP* 106p147, 1984), may be associated with the 'circular entrenchment on top' observed by Gough (Hutchins 1796-1814 4p318) and Charles Warne, but not by the Ordnance Survey or anyone else since. 'As old as Duncliffe Hill' was 'a North Dorset way of expressing anything particularly old' (Udal p294), just as Eggardon is in the west of the county. Barnes versifies the saying:
   'A mossy house, with bulging wall,
      Or door or window fall'n awry,
   Or oak that leant as if to fall,
      Or elm that now began to die,
   Or coat well kept through half a life,
      Or some old gown of some good wife,
   Of shape that now no more was rife
      Was called 'as old as Duncliffe Hill' (Barnes 1962 2p857).
More homely poets were concerned chiefly with the weather:
   'If Duncliffe Wood be fair and clear,
   You Stour Boys need have no fear.
   But if Duncliffe Wood do wear its cap
   You Marnhull folk look out for that' (Marnhull 1940 p114).
   These weather rhymes, based on the ending *cap-that*, are common throughout the British Isles, generally referring to some prominent local hill. Melbury Beacon was similarly used as a predictor of weather.

Dungeon Hill   Hillfort: Buckland Newton

In 1920 OI. G. S. Crawford interviewed a Buckland Newton man who had moved to the Isle of Wight, and who told 'a legend connected with Dungeon, a hill with an entrenchment ... affirming that a well is there with a golden table lying in the bottom. 'They' once tried to get it up, but this caused the foundations of a house nearby to shake, and the attempt was abondoned' (*SDNQ* 16p298, 1920).

Eggardon   Hillfort: Askerwell/Powerstock

There are two traditions about a Wild Hunt over this hill. In a newspaper of about 1953 appeared 'an account of a man's being pursued over Eggardon by the Devil. The man had

Dungeon Hill *and the* Vale *of* Blackmore.

The hillfort of Dungeon Hill, on the northern edge of the chalklands, drawn by Charles Harper in *The Hardy Country*, 1904.

made a bargain with the Devil for his soul, and the identity of the pursuer was known by the sparks issuing from his boots'. The informant, Mr. Harry Poole of Powerstock, said later, in 1974, that he 'had heard locally that Eggardon was haunted by Diana and her hounds, collecting the souls of the dead' (Waring 1977 p13).

The hill continues to have an uncanny reputation. Recently, Mr. Poole has described the finding of a circle of chicken feathers, supposed to be the remains of a sacrifice, and the apparent disturbing of some burial urns and scattering of their contents. Similar incidents have been reported from Abbotsbury Castle and Knowlton, but are probably the work of vandalism without any folklore content. Mr. Poole also describes a personal incident: he was working with a bill-hook on some hedges to the north of the hill, when he 'could hear a voice calling, but I never found anyone.Every time I stopped to listen the voice came from a different direction, a different part of the fog, and in the end I gave it up and went back to my hedging'. A few hours later, there was a sudden chill in the atmosphere, and in a momentary lapse of concentration he slipped with the bill-hook and cut an artery in his left wrist.

An incident of September 1974 was widely reported in the local and ufological press. A man was driving along the road past the monument when a ball of bluish light appeared ahead of him in the sky, and his car engine stalled; when the light moved off, his car was able to go again. 'Travellers along the old Roman road, or northwards towards Toller, have experienced temporary engine failure. Ten years ago, four cars stopped simultaneously, if I have understood the report correctly. It was still light and the engines refused to go for twenty minutes, when everything returned to normal' (Mr. H. S. Poole, Powerstock 1977)' (Waring 1977 p80). In 1983 traditions of the stopping of these cars and the appearance of the blue light have been collected from oral tradition.

A letter written by William Stukeley in 1709, to Roger Gale, mentions a local proverb for anything old, 'it is as old as Eggardon' (Quoted in Warne 1872 p221). The same saying was remembered in 1892 by H. J. Moule as one of the pet expresions of his childhood nurse,a

Cerne Abbas woman: 'Any very ancient thing was . . . Wull's Aggern' '(*SDNQ* 3p27, 1892).

Various traditions have been recorded about the octagonal enclosures within the hillfort (there is a map and excavation report in *DP* 100p55,1964). Warne says it was 'prepared for a plantation, to serve as a landmark for the channel, for a direction of certain vessels engaged in contraband trade, when homeward bound'. King's Farm, or North Eggardon House, was owned by Isaac Gulliver, who made the enclosure. 'He became celebrated as a contrabandist, and of his 'dealings and doings', so many anecdotes are still remembered, that . . . his deeds are likely to remain traditionary in Dorset' (Warne 1872 p59). In 1900, when the Field Club visited Eggardon, Gulliver had become 'a noted smuggler', but the story was still current, and was given to them by the occupant of King's Farm, repeating what his father, born there in 1810, had told him: 'The octagonal ditch and bank were made to protect a plantation . . . The Government, it is said, destroyed the plantation' (*DP* 21 pxxviii, 1900).

Further traditions about Gulliver were set down by the occupant of King's Farm in 1925. 'The cargoes were received by farm carts, and run inland on dark nights; and very often are said to have made for the 'King's House' (North Eggardon House) before being transferred to pack-horses and taken inland. For the purpose of temporary concealment these packages were sometimes hidden in large holes or caves dug in the hillside, of which traces were found as recently as 20 years ago at the back of my house, when a couple of horses engaged in ploughing disappeared into one of these pits, and had to be dug out'. This, though not necessarily connected with the hillfort, suggests some interesting possibilities for excavation.

There was a gallows here, as appears from a forest perambulation of 1300 which includes a stretch 'along the king's highway to *Wrechebergwe*; from there to the gateway of Eggardon castle on the eastern side; then through the middle of the castle as far as the gallows; from there to a ditch' (Hutchins 1861-70 2p317).

Eggardon was the scene of a bonfire in the Jubilee celebrations of 1897.

Gallows Hill   Round barrow: G. 11: Bere Regis

The site appears as Gallis Hill in 1682 and Gallows Hill in 1811. The gallows must have stood on the barrow, which occupies the highest ground on the hill; it has a fine view north to Woodbury, and perhaps the sight of it was intended to act as a deterrent to the pickpockets and petty thieves at the fair. The area still has a bad reputation. 'It's one of those places where people kill themselves', I was told (1984).

Giant's Grave   Rectangular mound: Melcombe Horsey

'There is a long mound in a part of my parish which is popularly called the 'Giant's Grave', and very near it two large stones . . . There is a popular tradition existing, though my informant somewhat doubted its correctness, that these stones move whenever they hear the cocks crow in Cheesilborne' (C. W. Bingham, in *Notes and Queries* 3rd ser. 9p10, 1866).

'Two giants standing on *Norden* (an adjacent hill) were once contending for the mastery as to which of them would hurl the furthest, the direction being across the valley towards *Hanging Hill*. He whose stone fell short was so mortified at the failure that he died of vexation, and was buried beneath the mound which has since been known as 'The Giant's Grave' ' (Warne in *Notes and Queries* p187).

The stones, as Bingham suspected, are natural rock outcrops. The legends appear to have grown around the naming of the mound as the Giant's Grave, the usual expression for long mounds.

The Giant's Grave and Trencher Barrows or pillow mounds: G. 1, 2:
Swanage

These are first heard of as 'a barrow on Ballard Down . . . called the 'Giant's' Grave' ' (Warne 1872 p325), or, 'Two low barrows known as the Giant's Grave' (Hutchins 1861-70 1p689). The two mounds are called the Giant's Grave and Trencher on the 1902 OS, and have been so known since. Their appearance as the Giant's Grave and *Stretcher* (Grinsell 1976) is presumably an alteration by association with ideas of burial, either a folklore variant or a printer's error.

It is quite common for hollows, usually natural, to be identified as the domestic equipment of legendary figures. In Dorset there is the Devil's Spoon and Trencher noted above, and the natural hollows in the heath at Affpuddle called Culpepper's Dish and Spoon. Elsewhere the Devil has a Punchbowl (Sussex), a Tinderbox Stonehouse Glos.), and a Frying-pan (Cadgwith, Cornwall); a giantess has a Cradle at Crud y Gawres, Ardudwy; even King Arthur has a Cup and Saucer at Tintagel.

The Grey Mare and her Colts Long barrow: G. IV: Long Bredy

The site is so called in Hutchins (1796-1804). The name 'Grey Mare' ocurrs in placenames elsewhere: there is a waterfall above Moffat in the Borders called the Grey Mare's Tail, and likewise a tower built at Warkworth Castle about 1260 was The Grey Mare's Tail. There may have been a legendary figure of this name, commemorated in Tom Pierce's grey mare at Widdecombe or the Welsh Mari Llwyd, but evidence is lacking. There are other stones with analogous names: at Haltwhistle (Northumberland) two standing stones are the Mare and Foal: some natural rocks in Pembrokeshire are the Devil's Nags; and a hollowed stone at Locronon (Finistère), which conferred fertility, was the Stone Mare. Again, there are parallels for the naming of rocks after animal family groups: rocks at Ilkley were called the Bull, Cow, and Calf, and the Cow and Calf, as well as being the term for Lewesdon and Pilsdon, is used to describe some rock groups off the shores of Devon.

The Grey Mare may be the barrow referred to by an informant who said that a solid golden coffin was buried in a barrow at Gorwell (*Dorset* 58p15, 1976).

Grimberry ?Barrow Corfe Castle
'Barrow haunted by a *grim* or goblin'. Three fields bearing this name are shown on an estate map of 1772; they run from 966.838 to 968.834 (DRO:D86/E16).

Grim's Ditch Entrenchment Cranborne/Pentridge/West Woodyates
An earlier name for Bokerley Dyke, meaning 'the ditch of *Grimr,* the hooded one'. Grim was one of the bynames of Odin, and presumably also of the English Woden, referring to the god's custom of walking on earth wrapped up in disguise; there may be some connection with modern hooded apparitions such as phantom monks. The name evidently lost its pagan connotations, for it is found as far west as Grimspound in Dartmoor, an area settled by the West Saxons long after they became Christian.

The bounds of Cranborne Chase in 1280 included a stretch 'from Chetell's Head to Grymsditch, and from Grymsditch to Handley' (Hutchins 1861-70 3p 407). 'Over

The Grey Mare and her Colts, in a tourist's sketch from the *Gentleman's Magazine* of 1815.

Blackdon hill (west of Merton) there runnes a great crooked Ditch, which comes from Cranborne-chase. J. Golden told me, 'tis called *Grimsditch*... It parts Dorsetshire & Wiltshire' (Aubrey 1665-93 p894). Hutchins calls it 'Grime Ditch or Boccoli ditch... This name is sometimes but improperly given to the Roman way' (1774 2p 221). The name is now extinct, but survives in the nearby Grim's Ditch parting Hampshire and Wiltshire, and the smaller Grim's Ditch in Martin.

Halstock   Roman pavement
When a Roman mosaic was found in the parish in 1830, Lord Ilchester cleared it and built a house over it. 'Some of the villagers, under the idea that treasures were secreted beneath, broke open the house at night and destroyed most of the pavement' (Hutchins 1861-70 4p 465).

Hambledon Hill   Hillfort   Child Okeford
'Two low barrows on Hamel-dun' were called Giant's Grave 'Warne 1872 p325). These would be G.1 and 2.

'An informant from Stourpaine indicated that the old hill forts of Hod and Hambledon hills protected the villages of Durweston and Stourpaine that lie close to these hills by some supernatural force...

'The ghost of a Roman centurion is said to haunt both Hod and Hambledon Hills...

'Hambledon Hill in Dorset has a dense yew forest that has produced a number of traditions explaining its origin. Generally held to be an unlucky place, some say that it was planted by the druids as a place in which to worship, others that it was planted by archers in later years to provide a ready supply of wood for their bows' (Palmer 1973 p21, 158, 79). In one variant, it is said that the bows used at the battle of Agincourt came from this wood.

A bonfire was lit on this hill for the Jubilee celebrations in 1897.

Hardown Hill barrows   Round barrows: G.1-6   Whitchurch Canonicorum
A bronze Age barrow group into which several intrusive Saxon burials appear to have been made (DP 53p 247, 1931; 90p 233, 1968). One local form of the name, unfortunately recorded at a late date (*Bridport News* 12 Sept. 1884) is Harrow-down, which suggests that the placename may include OE *hearg*, 'heathen temple'.

'Haddon beacon' is shown on William Kip's map of Dorset in 1612 (Shipp Collection 2fol1 , in DCM). The monument listed as Grinsell 6b and identified as a disc barrow by the Royal Commision (1p 265) consists of a circular bank surrounded by a ditch, enclosing a space in which there is a central mound, and connecting four symmetrically placed smaller circular banks. It is discussed in *DP* 90p 239, 1968; most probably it is the earthwork round a beacon, with the inner mound built up around its main post and the four rings left by the sockets of its supporting arms.

Hasler barrow   Round barrow: ?G.1   Steeple
'About a quarter of a mile north-west of Steeple are two or three grounds called *Hasler*. In one of them is a barrow, overgrown with hazel-wood, from the plenty of which hereabout the hundred takes its name. Here the hundred court was formerly held, but at present nearer Corfe' (Hutchins 1774 1p 193). The wood is named on the 1888 OS : it lies at 905.815.

The Hell Stone   Chambered long barrow: G.11   Portesham
'The common people call it *Hell Stone*, and have a tradition, that the devil flung it from Portland Pike, a north point of that island full in view, as he was diverting himself at quoits' (Hutchins 1774 1p 554). H. J. Moule (*Folk-Lore Journal* 6p 115) gave this tradition as if it were still current in 1888, but he may simply have repeated Hutchins; certainly all subsequent tellings of the story are only repetitions from the county history.

The name Hell Stone has attracted a great deal of speculative etymology, of which the Devil story represents a popular form. Antiquaries have, following Hutchins' original suggestions, derived the name from *halig*, 'holy'; from *heal*, 'to cover or conceal'; or from Hela in Scandinavian mytholoy. An argument from analogy would compare the Hell Stone with a group of other named dolmens such as Shilstone (now Spinsters' Rock) at Drewsteignton (Devon); a group of other Shilstones in Devon, where the monuments do not now survive; and Shelving-stone, a lost part of the Avebury complex. All these derive from *scylf*, 'shelf'. Similarly, the Hell Stone may derive from dialect *heal*, used for such actions as covering plants with earth or roofing a house with tiles. The word *hellyer* for 'tiler' is common in Dorset borough records, and *helling stones* for 'tiles' occurs in Dorset and Devon. The EDD does not record *heal* as a noun, but it so appears in an inscription of 1560 at Tisbury which refers to the church roof as 'this hele' (DP 15p. xxxiii, 1894).

The similar name of the Helstone at Longbredy remains unexplained, since this is a standing stone, or in, Warne's words, 'a rude unshapely gibbous mass' (1872p 111). The name Hell-Stone for this 'very large stone, eight or ten feet high' first occurs in Hutchins (1774 1p 295).

Lethbridge made an ambitious attempt to link up Hel- and El- elements in Dorset placenames with Helith, the supposed name of the Cerne Giant. His argument, like that of Piggott, is made invalid by the equation of the name *Helith* in Gotselin's life of St. Augustine, with the Cerne figure. In fact Gotselin merely says that a god Helith was formerly worshipped in Dorset– '*in quo pagus olim deus Helith colebatur*'.

Hod Hill   Hillfort   Stoupaine
Two traditions about this site have been given under the entry for Hambledon Hill.
A large number of Anglo-Saxon coins have recently been found to the east of this monument. Nine of them were sceattas (one dated to the eighth century and another, more precisely, to the second quarter of that century), and one was a penny of Offa (757-796). The penny must have come from Mercia, while one of the sceattas has the design of a Southampton mint. Seven of the coins lay to the west of the Iwerne Brook, on the Hanford side, and three to the east on the Stourpaine side, in the neighbourhood of Lazerton farm; the farm itself is of an ancient date, if it is to be identified with one of the Domesday manors of *Werne*. Although the coins were all found on the low ground by the river, it must be significant that the site lies just below Hod Hill. Perhaps the hillfort was the scene of some religious festival or administrative gathering that attracted people from round about, and an accompanying fair was held on the lower ground by Lazerton. (The coins are described in *DP* 101p 138 and 140, 1979; 103p 127, 1981; 105p 151, 1983).
'In the mid-1950s, when John Brailsford was digging with Sir Ian Richmond at Hod Hill, local people visiting the excavations spoke of a golden coffin as being buried there. (Information from L. V. Grinsell, 1975-7)' (Waring 1977 p54).
A bonfire was lit here for the Jubilee celebration in 1897.

Hundred Barrow   Round barrow: G.27   Bere Regis
'A place called Hundredes Barrowe' in 1593, this was originally the meeting-place for Bere Regis Hundred, and continued in use for the later area of Hundredsbarrow Hundred, which first appears as *Hundredesberihdr* in 1168.

Jeffrey and Jone   Standing stones (destroyed).   Portesham
'A little north of Hell Stone near Blagdon are four upright stones, near to, and equally distant from each other, about two feet high, except that one is broke off even with the ground. The common people preserve this obscure distich relating to it,
'Jefferey and Jone,
And their little dog Denty and Edy alone' (Hutchins 1774 1p 555).
In the synoptical index to Celtic Tumuli (1866p 20), written in 1865. Warne records the destruction of this monument: 'In a small valley, on the down of Portesham Farm, there stood within these last ten years, four upright stones ... By the direction of the then occupier of the farm, Mr. Manfield, these stones were built into an adjoining wall'. The monument must therefore have been destroyed about 1855. Its site is recorded on the 1888 O.S.
However, H. Colley March tells a variant account of their destuction. 'Warne says they have been built into an adjacent wall: but a man who was present at the ceremony stated that, by the spot where they once stood, a hole was made for them, and they were decently interred. The place where they are said to lie can be pointed out, as well as a wall which contains four large stones' (DP 29p. lxxiv, 1908). Colley March lived in Portesham, so his evidence carries some weight.
If the four stones were in fact buried, it may be possible at some date to excavate the site and set them up again. The suggestion of 'ceremony' in the burial of the stones is interesting: it seems as if, in contradiction to the will of the farmer, his workmen felt they should treat the monument with respect, even as they destroyed it. The burying of stones may be a late survival of mediaeval practice, since the stone-burials at Avebury are generally agreed to have had ceremonial as well as practical value.

A romantic watercolour of Hod Hill by John Baverstock Knight (1783-1859). He made a special note of 'the Bloody Field in the foreground, where many relics were found and battles fought'.

Kingston Down   Romano-British settlement   Corfe Castle

On Kingston Down above Chapman's Pool, 'recently a gold solidus of Theodosius was found here, and one man recalls how, in his younger days, on some late-night, unnamed errand, he hid shivering as a band of men marched by. Perhaps he feared a squadron of Preventive men, but the moonlight showed him legionaries of the Roman army on an anachronistic mission. Not long ago a small boy saw the same sight in daylight; his mother, seeing nothing, asked him what had frightened him, and he described the soldiers in detail, down to the metal fringes on their tunics' (Hyland 1978 p199).

It may be relevant that Chapman's Pool was originally *Schortmannes Poole,* and this 'short man' has been supposed to be some kind of dwarf or goblin. But there are other interpretations.

Knowlton Ring   Henge   Woodlands

The church that lies within the best-preserved of the earthworks is first mentioned in 1145 as a chapelry to the church at Horton, and continued to serve the hamlet of Knowlton until the ecclesiastical parishes of Knowlton and Horton were united in 1657-9. This was followed by 'an endeavour to pull down the parish church or chappel of Knolton and dispose of the materials' (*SDNQ* 1p 68, 1888; DP 36p 95, 1915). After this 'it lay unfrequented many years' until an attempted repair in about 1730, which cannot have been very thorough; 'the roof afterwards fell in, and the bell was taken away by some people of Sturminster-Marshal' (Hutchins 1774 2p 60). Since that time the church has been in ruins; it used to be clothed by a dark growth of ivy which impressed all visitors with a sense of gloom, but since about 1960 the Department of the Environment have rendered the site neat and sterile.

'A fair was formerly kept here, which has about forty years since been removed to Woodlands, where it is held July 5' (Hutchins 1774 2p 59). This was presumably held within the earthwork.

The group of four earthworks were probably taken for the remnants of a deserted village or town, with churches in each enclosure. This would explain the tradition given to William Stukeley by 'the landlady of the Rose Inn at Gussage All Saints in Cranborne Chase who, 'after some discourse preparatory', told him a muddled tale about Roman remains and the legend of the seven churches of Knowlton, and ended by pointing to the tale of Troy 'described in the ballad upon her wall, where she showed me these passionate verses, 'Waste lie those walls that were so good/And corn now grows where Troy towers stood' '(Piggott 1950 p74, quoting the *Itinerarium Curiosum).* A century later, 'the peasantry have a legend relating how a large number of churches in ancient times stood in this neighbourhood, and this is no doubt the tradition to which Stukeley alludes' (Warne, 1872 p103). The theft of the bell by Sturminster men has given rise to a large body of tradition incorporating traditional elements (the bell was lost in a pool, and could not be dragged to land again after someone made a blasphemous brag); there is a similar group of stories told about the loss of Bindon bells.

The modern beliefs about the site are mostly inspired by its eerie qualities, especially the scrub growth there – 'Elder, superstition says, thrives about the bones of the dead' *(Dorset Countryside* 11 p21, 1970). 'The place is magical, and said to be haunted. The ditch is inside the rampart... to prevent the egress of the spirits confined within, rather than for defense. The ruined church, recently cleared of scrub and blackthorn, stands in the centre of a well-kept sward. A few old yews are left' (Pitt-Rivers 1966 p87). No clear statement has been made about this haunting, and there is as little evidence for the rumoured practice of black magic at the site: 'A could of years ago there was a suspicious patch of burnt grass on the downs above Abbotsbury... There are repeated rumours of similar activities in the ruins of the Norman church at Knowlton' *(Dorset* 39 p29). These hints and allusions are without foundation – 'a suspicious patch of burnt grass'! – but they have acquired some currency, and reflect popular attitudes to the place.

Lambert's Castle   Hillfort   Marshwood

'Upon what ground I could never yet learne, the Countrie People will shew you an Hole near the toppe of the Hill, of which they will tell you more Fables than I list to write ... of the Spirits haunting that Place' (Gerard 1630 p14). These 'fonde Opinions, which no man can turne them from' are compared in number to the accounts of demons in the life of St. Guthlac: and although this may merely be a scholarly comparison, it is noteworthy that Guthlac's tormentors also frequented a prehistoric monument, a barrow at Croyland. They were coarse, ragged, deformed creatures, who may have had more of the outlaw than the devil in their make-up.

According to a memorandum of 1832, from the Hawkchurch register, 'there are at present holden on Lambert's Castle two annual fairs, the one in the month of June, for which a charter was granted by Henry VI, of some consequence – a few years since it was celebrated for the excellence of its races, wrestling, and other manly sports, and it not unfrequently happened that they were graced by forty or fifty equipages of the neighbouring gentry; but latterly, owing to various causes, few persons of any consequence attend the fair, and it is holden chiefly for the sale of cattle. The fair is always on the third Wednesday and Thursday in June, but it has been changed, very unwisely, from the days mentioned in the charter' *(SDNQ* 5 p238, 1896).

Hutchins is brief on this subject: '7 Anne, a grant passed, to hold a fair yearly, on certain hills, called Lambert's-Castle and Hawkchurch-Down, on the Wednesday before the feast of St. John the Baptist' (1774 1p330). The third edition expands on this: the fair was on the first Wednesday before Old Midsummer Day, the feast of St. John, who was formerly patron saint of Hawkchurch. The first fair (apparently that granted by Henry VI) was 'for all kinds of cattle and merchandise'; the second (apparently from the charter of Queen Anne) was held nine weeks later. Tolls were taken of both for the manor of Abbot's Wootton. 'Little business is now done at these fairs, but they are still much frequented as holydays for the country people of the neighbourhood' (Hutchins 1861-70 4p51).

In the later 19th century, the popular games gradually became resticted to horse racing, which was much patronised by the gentry, and up to 1947 it could be said that 'annual horse races keep green the memory of its mediaeval fair' (Turner 1947).

'Tradition also has it that women with pikes drilled at the top of Lambert's Castle, 'to frighten away the French' ' (Dacombe 1935 p20). This is one of many traditions about women dressed as soldiers frightening off the enemy: in the type-specimen of the legend, at Fishguard (Pembrokeshire), the women wore red cloaks and were taken for soldiers. The same story occurs at Ilfracombe and Lyme.

Loosebarrow   Barrow: G.5.   Morden

A barrow in this parish was the meeting-place for a Hundred, known as *Celeberge* in 1086 and as *Luseberge* in 1130. That the two names refer to a single site is shown by Hutchins' reference: 'Loosebarrow, where the hundred courts were formerly kept, stands... near the west end of Charborough Down, but the barrow now is almost levelled' (Hutchins 1774 2p182).

The site appears as a 'planted barrow' on a map of the park by Isaac Taylor, drawn 1773-7 (DRO); it lies at 917.982, on a knoll by the park boundary. Shipp in his edition of Hutchins describes some fifteen Romano-British burials found in 1810 on opening a large barrow 'towards the west end of Charborough Down... in order to put in some good earth for planting flowering shurbs' (Hutchins 1861-70 3p505. Another group of Romano-British finds nearby is noted in DP 85p105, 1963).

Maiden Castle   Hillfort   Winterborne St. Martin
This monument, first named in a 1600 edition of Camden, is the largest, southernmost and most famous of an extensive group of earthworks called Maiden Castle, Bower, or some such variant. A tour from north to south of Britain would include the following instances:-

In Scotland there are Maiden Castles at Oyne (Aberdeenshire); at Falkland and at Kennoway (Fifeshire); and at Falkirk (Stirling). The name *Castellum Puellarum* for Edinburgh first appears in 1142, and its usage in Geoffrey of Monmouth may mean it was current in the 1130s. The *Chronicle of Lanercost,* under the year 1296, says the city 'is called Edwynesburgh from its royal founder, King Edwyn; here he is said to have placed his seven daughters to keep them in safety'. The name is rendered as *Chastel des Pucelles* and the *Castle of Maydens* in the later redactions of the Matter of Britain, but the romancers do not add anything helpful on its meaning.

There is a large group of sites in north-western England. In Westmorland, Maiden-hold (1777) in Appleby St. Michael is a small Roman camp. Mayburgh *(Maburgh* 1671) in

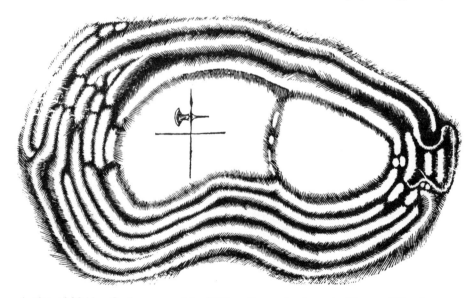

A plan of Maiden Castle, engraved by William Barnes for Savage's *History of Dorchester,* 1833.

Barton has been identified as an amphitheatre. Maiden Castel (1823) at Low Abbey in Kirkby Thore may have been an earthwork; and in the same parish Maborough Castle (1750) is an entrenchment by the 12th-century Whelps Castle. *Mayden Castel* (1540) in Stainmore is a Roman fort, occupied from the late second to the fourth centuries; there may be an earlier form of the name from 1292 (See *Tr. of the Cumberland and Westmorland Antiquarian Soc.* 27p 170). The henge called Mayburgh in Yanwath & Eamont Bridge is first recorded in 1789 (CWAS 12p153).

In Cumberland, the tenants of the manor of Eskdale were required in 1587 to bring their cattle 'at Beltan time... to Maidencastle'. This is 'a rude enclosure beside the track from Burnmoor Tarn to Wasdalehead', with a tradition of use as a beacon (CWAS 22p 77). Mawbray in Holme St. Cuthbert *(Mayburg'* 1175) is a Roman fort. Maiden Castle has now replaced Carthannock as the name of an earthwork on Soulby Fell in Matterdale; the site is in fact indefensible, being overlooked by two hills. 'My grandfather... born at Wreay in 1797, used to tell the following story of the Soulby Maiden Castle: it was originally, according to his account, a tower built by a king for the preservation of his daughter, whose death by drowning has been prophesied by a malignant fairy godmother. The princess grew up in safety, but as she was in the act of eloping with a lover, by means of a window, she slipped and fell into the water-butt' (CWAS 12p 143). An inquisition of 1286 was made 'at Maydencastel in the Forest of Englewode', and this refers either to the Matterdale site or to Maiden Hill just north of Penrith, where an old watch-tower stood *(CWAS* 6p 162; 26p 56). A probable hillfort, 'Maiden Castle' in 1923, was recorded near Ulpha, north of Broughton in Furness *(CWAS* 23p 271).

In Northumberland the Maiden Castle hillfort at Earle & Wooler is mentioned in Burn's *History of Westmorland,* while 'a terrace now in the centre of Wooler was formerly called the Maiden Knowe' and there was a Maiden Walk near Wark Castle. It has been suggested that Carvoran on the Maiden Way (a Roman road running north from Kirkby Thore) was *Caer forwyn,* from Welsh *morwyn,* 'maiden' (Denham Tracts 2p 151). The name of the Maiden Way – *Maydengathe, Maidingate,* or *Maidengate* in references of 1179 and 1294 – has been associated with the other sites by R.C. Collingwood. A letter sent to Camden in 1601 says 'The maiden waie comes directlie to it from Caervorran, and so it goeth to maiden kirk wiche is distance some half mile from Whitley Castle... and so to maiden castle upon Staine more'. The *puellarum templum,* says the correspondent (lapsing in Latin) is now altogether destroyed (CWAS 11 p359; 30p 116).

In Co. Durham there is a Maiden Castle 'an old earthern fortress' east of Durham *(Denham Tracts* 2p 151) as well as a hill called Maiden Bower a mile west of the city (Bartholomew's Gazetteer). In Cheshire there is a Maiden Castle at Bickerton or Broxton. In Yorkshire one at Bowes – presumably the Norman castle there – is mentioned by Hutchins on the authority of Dr. Gale (1774 1p 467). At Grinton-on-Swale the name Maiden Castle was applied in 1823 to an enclosure of doubtful age and purpose; there is an avenue leading to the site, which is overlooked by a neighbouring hill (VCH Yorks. 2p 65). The entrenchment now called Becca Banks at Saxton was *Maidenecastell* in 1175-86. Maiden Bower at Topcliffe is another Norman castle, repaired by the Bishop of Lincoln in 1174 (VCH Yorks. 2p 40).

Moving further south, in Bedfordshire there is a Maiden Bower at Dunstable, and a Medbury *(Meidebir* 1227) in Elstow, though here there is no earthwork. In Cambridgeshire, Castle Mound to the north of Cambridge was *Maidenburg* in the 12th century; and the same name appears in some compound forms at Kneesworth, *Maidenberell'* in 1493 and *Maidenberiweye* in 1513, though no earthwork survives. In Essex, Maidenburgh

Street in Colchester was *Maydeneburgh* in 1248. In Oxfordshire, Maiden Bower in Steeple Barton is recorded by Gough (Hutchins 1796-1814 3p 194). In Gloucestershire, *Maydes Castle* occurs as a fieldname of 1667 at Aston Subedge, but no monument has been identified. And finally comes Maiden Bower, an island 1½ miles west of Bryher in the Scillies (Bartholomew). This list has been derived from Allcroft, Grinsell 1976, Wheeler and the relevant volumes of the English Place-Name Society as well as the other authorities cited.

As Hutchins (1774 1p 467) remarks, the names 'occur in several places in the North of England', forming a disproportionate cluster there. Of the 38 forms listed, five are Scots, one Cornish and the rest English. In England, 24 occur north of the Trent and only 8 south of it; the northern examples belong mostly to Cumbria, with a distinct grouping around Penrith, while in southern England there is a cluster in Bedfordshire, Cambridgeshire and Essex. The Dorset, Gloucestershire and Oxfordshire instances, like that in the Scillies, are isolated exceptions. The cluster of six in Westmorland and five in Cumberland may be an example of that anomalous regional specialisation in certain sorts of folklore which is implied by the high local concentrations of legends – eg. stories of supernatural church movements in Cornwall or of dragon-slaying on the Quantocks, both far above the national average. In any case, the distribution of sites shows that Maiden names are a distinctly northern form, and that the Dorset site is an isolated southern outlier of the group.

The chronological evidence shows that Maiden names were being applied to sites (and therefore had some meaning to their users) well into the mediaeval period. For one thing, Falkirk, Topcliffe and Cambridge Castle Hill are mediaeval castles, and so presumably are the Kikby Thore and Bowes sites; they cannot have received their name until after they had been built and fallen into ruin. For another, the large number of Maiden *Castles* implies that the name was given after the Conquest. All the Scottish instances are called Castle. In England *castel* forms occur 14 times and *burh* forms 12 times, plus the Cornish instance; there are also a Hold, Knowe, Walk, Kirk and Way associated with the Maidens. All the East Midland group are *burh* forms, while both types of name occur in the Cumbrian cluster.

The earliest forms come from the 12th century – Edinburgh in the 1130s, Holme St. Cuthbert in 1175, Saxton in 1175-86, and the Maiden Way in 1179. Maiden Castle continued to be recorded from the 16th to the 19th century, but these names were probably given at an earlier date. The absence of the English name from the borders of Wales and the Highlands suggests that it was obsolete when English began to oust the Celtic languages here, although it was able to displace the Cumbrian name Carthannock in Matterdale.

The topography of Maiden– sites does not offer any clue to the meaning of the name. At six sites no earthwork has been identified, suggesting either a transferred name or a monument so slight that it has vanished since the Middle Ages. The identified sites are a motley group of hillforts, Roman camps, castles, and at Saxton a boundary dyke. Few of them have the appearance of prominent or secure fortresses.

There are similar names in other languages. Wheeler has compared Magdeburg in Germany (whose name goes back to the 9th century) with the Maiden Bower forms, and cites a Byzantine fortress in Macedonia called Avret Hissar or Gunaicocastro, and a 5th-century ecclesiastical settlement in northern Syria called Qasr-el-Banat, both names meaning 'castle of maidens' (Wheeler 1943 p10). Grinsell (1976 p72) refers to four fortlets in the Hebrides, on Colonsay, Islay, Mull, and Tiree, called *Dun nan Nighean,* 'fort of the maidens'; there are legends here of maidens incarcerated in the forts. If the etymology of Carvoran in Northumberland be correct, the term existed at an early date in Welsh or British. All these places were within the cultural range of mediaeval romance, and the Middle Eastern forms may have been introduced by the Crusaders; but the Magdeburg form, if it belonged to this group, would argue for a Germanic origin, and certainly the earliest English names – including the *burh* forms at Holme St. Cuthbert (1175) and Cambridge (12th century) – are likely to antedate any influence from the romances.

There have been numerous attemps to explain the Maiden-names. The folk explanation is recorded by early an tourist: 'Maiden Castle, because they say it was never overcome' (Peter Munday's *Travels in Dorset,* 1635, in *DP* 42p 49, 1922); likewise in Gerard, 'this is called by the Countrie People Mayden Castle, upon a Tradition that it was never yet forced or wonne'. The local legends at Edinburgh and some of the other Scottish sites refer to maidens kept in the earthworks for one purpose or another. The OED suggests 'a fortress so strong as to be capable of being defended by maidens'. Wheeler proposes 'a refuge for women in time of war'. Smith quotes these four views, and adds a fifth, 'it is possible that such places were associated with games and the like in which maidens took part'.

So many of the sites are of slight or negligible strength, that the first and second of these interpretations can be discounted: they only show that the original sense of the name had been lost by 1600. The meaning of Maiden Castle can only be established by analogy with other Maiden–names. Many of these refer to ordinary girls: Maiden Lane occurs as a variant of Lover's Lane, and a Maiden Ford was one that could be easily crossed (Smith 1956 s.v.) But the group of sites called Maiden Well is too large to be so explained, since many of the sites lie at a distance from any centre of habitation. There was a *Maidenwelle* (1306) in Worth Matravers, and the form occurs in other counties – Maidenwell in Berkshire, Cornwall, Lincolnshire (1212) and Louth, and Maidwell in Northamptonshire *(Medewelle* 1086). Maidstone – *Maeidesstana* in the 10th century – is similarly unexplained, though the swelling hills of Maiden Paps (Caithness, Durham, and Roxburghshire; common in Ireland) require little interpretation.

It is probable that the element 'maiden' has some allusive or folkloristic sense here. *Lady* in mediaeval placenames refers to the Virgin Mary, as in *Levidiforhude* (1317) in Winterborne Whitchurch, whose church is dedicated to the Virgin; *Ladiclos* (1461) in Winfrith Newburgh; and Lady Well on the 1888 O.S., overlooking Abbotsbury Abbey. But there are no examples of 'maiden' being used in this sense.

Who were the maidens? Certainly by the 13th century the Maiden Castle names were being explained as 'fortress in which maidens were guarded' for some legendary reason, and it may be that the applications of the name to mediaeval sites carry this meaning. But since some of the earthworks are clearly indefensible – the Matterdale and Grinton-on-Swale monuments are overlooked by hills – an earlier meaning must have existed. Most other names of the form 'Such-and-such's monument' belong to supernatural beings – Grimsberry, Puckysbarry, and Thursdyche in this Inventory are examples – and imply a belief in the apparition of the *grima, puca* or *thyrs* at the place. It may be significant that the folklore of otherworldly beings on the Continent believes in a race of supernatural ladies, appearing as fees in France, fadas in Provence, nymphae in ancient and modern Greece, Seligen amongst the Germans, Vily amongst the Slavs, Rusalky in Russia. The description of the Rusalky will serve for all: they 'are very beautiful and have pale skin, white breasts, slender bodies, and beautiful long wavy hair. Their eyes are wild'. These lovely and aristocratic maidens haunt springs, stones, and trees, or live in the forests, and can do good to the peasant who claims one as a wife or a fairy godmother. There is nothing quite like them in Britain, where the fairy traditions take a different form: but there may have been in the Middle Ages. If so, then the Maiden castles, bowers, stones, well, roads, and so on would be natural or archaeological sites which had been believed to be haunted by these supernatural beings.

There are other traditions associating Maiden Castle in Winterborne St. Martin with legendary beings. 'Maiden Castle... was built by giants' (Waring 1977 p48, giving no source). An informant in 1982 (again, unfortunately, giving no source) told me he had read that fairy lights could at certain seasons be seen moving over the ramparts here. I was told of the following incident in 1983: according to my notes, the informant said that 'about eleven years ago, he and two or three other people had driven over in the moonlight to go for a walk. It was a November night. As they sat in the carpark, the car began to move up and down, starting slowly and then speeding up. It tilted at front and back, along its long axis, in a way that no animal could sway a car. They were looking out of the windows, so that if a person had been trying to move the car, they would have seen so. They didn't get out to investigate, being too scared, but drove off'. Another informant, during the writing of this paper, told me of an incident a few years ago when he was walking on the monument at night with a friend. She saw a group of Roman soldiers marching over the middle ground, and was clearly frightened by the experience, though he saw nothing. The same phenomenon of selective apparition has been reported from Kingston Down (see above).

These stories of apparitions would explain the belief, of which I was told in 1985, that no-one can ever spend a night up at Maiden Castle. Somehow or other, they are always forced to go down from it. Presumably they would be disturbed by a haunting such as that at Badbury. (Actually the site was permanently occupied during Wheeler's excavation).

There is one feature at this site which has given rise to legends and speculation. 'On the south side of this work is a place seemingly the mouth of a hollow cave, which some nice Observers will have to be an artificial thing; but for what use it should be contriv'd, is altogether uncertain' (Camden, ed. Gibson, col. 53). This was the scene of legend in Gerard's time – 'I think it will be needlesse for mee to mention an Hole neare the toppe of this Hill, of which the neighbour Inhabitants tell manie Stories not worth the relating' (Gerard 1630 p72). By the 18th century, the legend had reached its present form. 'Near the south entrance is the mouth of a cave, which the vulgar will have to be the entrance of a subterranean passage that led into the midst of Dorchester. Attentive observation shows it to be artificial' (Hutchins 1774 1p 467, citing an edition of Camden). These authorities are referring to the outcrop of conglomerate rock at 668.883, below the outer rampart, half-way along its southern side. This outcrop is slightly hollow underneath, and looks as if it might be the beginning of an arch or the entrance to a tunnel. 'Local tradition has it that beneath this stone lintel was found a stairway, and that after so much had been discovered, the staircase was filled up with earth' (Hubbard and Hubbard 1907 p39).

The legend of the tunnel is found independently of this structure. 'There is an old tradition of an underground passage from Dorchester to Maiden Castle' (Moule 1901 p7); Darton speaks of it as running 'from Maiden Castle to the Town Pump – two miles' (Darton 1935 p126), and the theme inspired a local poet in praise of Fordington Field:-

'O, Varntin Vield, th'wold volk zay
There's a tunnel to Dorchester, Ma'en Castle way
Yer Zecret up to now thou'ast kept very quiet
But, iv 'twere known, a Syndicate 'ould buy it...'. *(DYB* 1949-50p 106).

'I was told that a tunnel, two miles long, running from Dorchester to Maiden Castle, was used by the Home Guard in World War II. It goes from either the Market, the Junction Hotel, or the Town Pump' (Waring 1977 p50). And I have also been told that it emerges in the Borough Gardens.

One version of the story has it that a duck was put down the Maiden Castle entrance and emerged a few days later, looking slightly confused, in the centre of Dorchester; this detail of the duck is used in tunnel legends elsewhere.

Maiden Castle has recently become colonised by the new custom of dancing on hilltops on May Day. On 1st May 1985 the women's team from Portland, the Royal Manor Morris Dancers, turned up to perform dances from the traditional Cotswold repertoire as the sun rose; the performance, which claimed to revive a Dorset tradition, must have been inspired by the Wessex Morris Men at the Trendle in Cerne. It remains to be seen whether the custom will spread to the other hilltops which formerly saw popular gatherings on fair days or Good Friday. The Royal Manor team were supported by a crowd of about thirty, plus a lone protestor complaining, not very seriously, about the impending commercialisation of the monument *(Dorset Evening Echo* 1 May 1985).

There are two stories which associate Maiden Castle with games, or (what was equally often the scene of festivities in old Dorset) with a gallows. The newspapers of 1798 announced a round of rustic sports to be held on the monument on the 29th of September, in honour of the birthday of HRH the Duchess of Wurtemburgh, and to be attended by the Royal Family, come up from Weymouth for the morning. 'All persons of jovial, friendly, and loyal dispositions are invited to be present at, and to partake of, the undermentioned country sports...

A cheese to be rolled down the hill; prizes to whoever stops it...

A pound of tobacco to be grinned for..

A handsome hat, for the boy most expert in catching a roll dripped in treacle, and suspended by a string...

A pig; prize to whoever catches him by the tail' –

–and there were races on foot, and horse-racing, and cudgelling contest *(SDNQ* 5p 73)

According to correspondence in the *DCC* (28th March 1935), there was a gallows on Maiden Castle, afterwards removed to Bradford Down. E.A. Ramsden wrote in, giving details of its location on Bradford Down, and telling this story: 'Some local men, drinking in Dorchester on a winter's night, dared one of their number to carry a bowl of broth and offer it to the skeleton hanging on the gibbet there. He consented, and his companions, taking advantage of the dark night, sped over the fields and, getting there first, crouched down under the low wall behind the gibbet and waited in hiding.

'The broth-carrier arrived, and, holding up the bowl to the hanging figure, said 'Your broth, sir'. Whereupon a sepulchral voice, apparently from the gibbet, replied, 'Blow it, it's hot!' which so frightened the poor man that he dropped the bowl, fled shrieking, and never recovered his wits'.

The same story is told of a gallows at Shrewsbury (Burne 1887 p592).

Maumbury   Henge and amphitheatre   Dorchester (Fordington)

The folklore of this monument is of particular interest, for the purposes to which it has been put over the last three centuries suggest a continuity of use from Roman to modern Dorchester. The earlier Neolithic phase of the site, being unsuspected by the antiquaries, has left no impression on folklore; the ghosts here are Roman. 'Some old people said that at certain moments in the summer time, in broad daylight, persons sitting with a book, or dozing in the arena, had, on lifting their eyes, beheld the slopes lined with a gazing legion of Hadrian's soldiery as if watching the gladiatorial combat; and had heard the roar of their excited voices; that the scene would remain but a moment, like a lightning flash, and then disappear' *(The Mayor of Casterbridge* (1886) chap. 11.). This belief was recorded again in 1947, though doubtless influenced by the literary reference: 'there is a tradition that anyone who falls asleep when resting on the sloping grass mounds, will see phantoms of Roman soldiers drilling or engaged in combat' *(DYB* 1949-50 p10).

But most traditions about Maumbury refer to its use as a centre for popular gatherings of one sort or another. This use seems to go back to the 17th century, though it cannot antedate the use of the site as a military emplacement in the Civil War. H.J. Moule argued that the Rings had been used, or intended to be used, as a bull-ring. The 'great stone with a chain fastened to it', which is noted in Hutchins, was remembered by local people including the shepherd Nat Seal. 'It was said to be lying on the ground, or only partly covered. One day a plough belonging to Farmer Masters became entangled in the chain. To prevent this happening again the stone was buried at the entrance, Nat said'. Moule suggests that the stone originally stood at Bull-Stake, now North-Square, and had been moved in the 17th century when the town became too crowded to allow the violence of bull-baiting within its walls. If so, the stone can never have been used in its new location, for stones in bull-rings were always buried, with only a single ring (not a chain) showing at ground level. (Moule 1901 p6).

The gallows were put up here in the 18th century: they appear in a print of 1786 as a simple structure of two poles and a cross-bar, standing beside the north entrance. The most famous execution at the site was that of Mary Channing in 1705, who committed petty treason by poisoning her husband, and was sentenced to be strangled and then burnt in the centre of the Rings, with thousands of bystanders looking down from the terraces of the amphitheatre. 'Tradition reports that at a certain stage of the burning her heart burst and leapt out of her body, to the terror of them all, and that not one of those ten thousand people ever cared particularly for hot roast after that' *(Mayor of Casterbridge).* Tradition is probably unreliable, for the same detail of the bursting heart is found in one of Barham's *Ingoldsby Legends,* describing the burning of a witch in a place called Bloody-heart Lane. Channing has been identified as a witch herself; a travel writer says of the Leigh maze, 'the last witch in England (she was executed in Maumbury Rings in the late seventeenth century) is supposed to have been arrested while at a meeting here' (Hyams 1970 p223). The popular imagination, which always thinks of witchcraft suspects as being burned (they were in fact hanged) has incorporated Mary Channing into another set of stories.

An article in the *Times* (9 Oct. 1908) describes the violent demonstrations which took place at Maumbury in 1850 during 'the 'No Popery' riots... witnessed by this writer when a small child. Highly realistic effigies of the Pope and Cardinal Wiseman were borne in procession from Fordington Hill round the town, followed by a long train of mock priests monks, and nuns, and preceded by a young man discharging Roman candles, till the same wicked old place was reached, in the centre of which there stood a huge rick of furze, with a gallows above. The figures were slung up, and the fire blazed till they were blown to pieces by fireworks contained within them'. Later, in 1915, it could be said: 'we have used Maumbury as a place of public service, entertainment, or instruction on various occasions. At the Coronation of a king, for the protest against the Welsh Disestablishment Bill, or for a National Reservist parade, the Rings have been filled with spectators in the ancient manner' (Bartelot p31). There were united services by the Anglican and Free Church congregations on 'occasions such as victories of the South African war – Ladysmith relieved – Mafeking relieved – the Diamond Jubilee of Queen Victoria and the Coronation of King Edward VIII' *(DYB* 1955-6 p129). And when the Dorset Industry Exhibition opened in 1948, it began with 'balloons let off by the children from Maumbury Rings (produced by a Dorchester firm)' *(DYB* 1949-50 p158).

Maumbury also served as a sportsfield in the days when no public provision was made for such things, 'way back in the 20s and 30s'. Local boys belonged to three factions – those of Fordington to the east playing in Salisbury Fields, those living to the west of town who used Poundbury, and those on the south who played in Maumbury. A veteran of these football matches remembers, 'For the annual 'Whites' versus 'Blues' Maumbury Cup tussles I obtained permission from Dorchester Borough Council to erect mini goalposts and corner posts, also a certain amount of whitewash lime marking. This proved to be a real distinction because we became the only Dorchester Football Club to be granted this concession. These Good Friday matches were watched by quite large crowds from the natural 'grandstands' provided by the grassy slopes' *(DYB* 1983 p54). A photograph of one of these football matches between Whites and Blues in Maumbury is reproduced in the *Dorset Evening Echo,*18 Oct. 1984. The playing of games on Good Friday has been traditional since the later Middle Ages; there was an annual game of tipcat on this date held on the lynchets below the Cerne Giant (Darton 1935).

William Stukeley, speculating on the derivation of Maumbury (then pronounced *Mumury)* in his discourse offered to the Freemasons in 1723, thought it might come from the word 'mummer'. Alfred Pope later supported the same derivation, 'it being the place in which the local play actors are said to have carried on their 'frolicks' *(DP* 7p 67, 1885), and his tradition may be more reliable than his etymology. There have, at any rate, been modern mummers within the Rings. *Word and Action,* a company of players calling themselves 'a community (theatre and writing) service', promised in their 1978 handbill to perform here on Wednesday mornings in their 'Sumer Instant Theatre... festive plays for all the family to enjoy, the audience is given an opportunity to create and act out its own play. *Collection afterwards'.* The list of topics includes Instant Fairy Stories, Dorset Myths and Legends, Ghosts and Witches, and Horror Stories.

Maumbury standing amongst the wheat of Fordington Field, with the gallows to one side and the road passing by, from a sketch of 1755 in Grose's *Antiquities of England and Wales.*

65

Marnhull   Roman cemetery

Informants in 1931 said 'a funeral was supposed to be seen at midnight (on a certain date) crossing Sackmore Lane from Fillymead to Dunford's. There were no mourners following and the faces of the bearers were hidden beneath the pall which covered the coffin. 'It went along the line of the fighting'. This refers to the supposed battlefields near Todber, near to the quarry where so many human remains were found in 1870. The same story is told of Grove Field near Nash Court, which is practically in a line from Fillymead to Todber. A local explanation of the name Todber is 'Trod bare', ie. by the troops at the time of the fighting' *(Marnhull* 1940 p107).

These legends refer to the 'large quantities of human bones' found at various places in the parish when stone quarries were opened in the fields. In most cases the bodies were oriented, and lay without grave goods: in the finds at Great Down Quarry in 1870-1, the oriented bodies were associated with Roman remains, chiefly coins and brooches, with sherds of Samian and black-burnished ware (Hutchins 1861-70 4p 326).

Melbury Hill   Entrenchment   Melbury Abbas

The hill was used by people in the Shaftesbury area as a weather prognosticator; if it appeared closer than usual, or wore a 'cap' of mist, rain was on the way. Dorchester people make the same use of Hardy's Monument, and Lighthouse Rock is watched by Portlanders.

The domestic state papers of May 1588 describe the system of beacons as then planned: Melbury beacon was to be fired to give alarm to Wiltshire from the Dorset coast. The site appears on Sumner's map of the earthwork (Sumner 1913 p66-7). This beacon was used in the 1804 invasion scare, and for the 1897 celebrations.

Modbury   Round barrow   Sydling St. Nicholas

Modbury Hundred appears as *Morberca* in 1086, when it contained the later hundreds of Cerne and Totcombe. It takes its name from 'a barrow called Modbury, on the hill north of Catistock, between that and Cerne, where the hundred-court was formerly kept' (Hutchins 1774 2p 281). Gough in his additions to Hutchins tells us that the site lay a quarter of a mile from the Celtic field system on the slopes of The Combe (Hutchins 1796-1814 4p 304) and that 'old people say that (in perambulation) the boundaries of the parish towards Sydling were considered to extend a few feet beyond this barrow' (Hutchins 1796-1814 3p 295). The boundary of Cattistock and Sydling here coincides with the A37, more or less the same route as the Dorchester-Yeovil turnpike and the Roman road from Dorchester to Ilchester. It follows that the barrow must have lain near Staggs Folly. In the field east of the road here, on the Sydling side, there appears to have been a barrow at 616.003; it is utterly levelled by the plough, but a circular cluster of large flints shows where its core lay.

Modbury   ? Barrow   Swyre

Modbury Farm, at the north-western corner of the parish, is described by Hutchins as 'an hamlet... where ruins and foundations appear on both sides of the road that leads to Burton, under a cover of trees', and he identifies it with the early form *Motberge* (1774 1p 570). This was apparently a 13th-century settlement; pottery of that date has been noted on the site (DP 87p 92) and the earliest form of the name occurs in 1236 (Fägersten 1933 p252). The barrow from which the hamlet took its name must have lain near the boundary of Burton, Sturthill and Swyre manors, but it was not a hundredal moot; perhaps the people in the Bride Valley had arranged for informal gatherings to be held there to settle their common problems. A similar explanation is required by the name of Motcombe parish in the north-east of the county.

Motbeorh   ?Barrow: G. Longbredy 17a   Abbotsbury

This site is mentioned in the Portesham charter of 1024 *(DP* 59p 114, 1937). From the details of the boundary, it would seem to be close to the junction of Abbotsbury, Longbredy, and Portesham parishes at the ridgeway, which appears in the charter as a *straet;* formerly Littlebredy parish, which now ends a hundred yards away, probably extended to this junction. The nearest barrow to meet the terms of the charter is Abbotsbury 20, although Grinsell numbers the site as Longbredy 17a. It seems likely that the steep bottom to the south of the road here was the original Ucga's Combe which gave name to Uggescombe Hundred, although Hutchins would identify that site with a Mystecombe a little to the east in Portesham.

At the parish junction, where the metalled part of the ridgeway ends, is a gate at the meeting-point of some ancient hedges, and besides the gate is a small pudding-stone, about a foot and a half in diameter. This was identified by Sandra Harding, of Portesham school, as a Moot Stone (I had reached the same conclusion myself from the Abbotsbury side of the boundary): it may be a mediaeval boundstone, but its existence in an area where there are several megalithic monuments, including pudding-stones, is noteworthy. The stone is not now earthfast, as people have had to turn it over to get vehicles in and out of the gate.

Motborow   Barrow; unlocated   Puddletown

The Hundred of Puddletown met at an unlocated site called *Modbergh* in 1404 and *Motborow* in 1531.

Nine-barrow Down   Round barrows; G. 11-20b   Corfe Castle

'So called, from some of the largest and highest, though they are ten in number' (Hutchins, in the *Gentleman's Magazine* 1768 p109). Warne was told that Whitecliffe was 'the scene of a terrible fight, in which nine kings were slain, all of whom were buried in a group of tumuli on Nine Barrow Down' (Warne 1872 p239).

The actual number remains in dispute. Hutchins, on a second reckoning, counted sixteen (1774 1p 185); Rodney Legg made out seventeen, but notes that only nine are over two feet high; he gives the tradition of the nine kings as still current (Legg 1972 p108). Mills was told that 'according to local information there were originally nineteen'. It is clear, at any rate, that nine is a merely conventional number.

The Nine Stones   Stone circle   Winterbourne Abbas

This monument was also known as the Nine Ladies or the Devil's Nine Stones *(DP* 29p. lxxiv. 1908). In 1941 they were associated with the Devil and with human sacrifice *(SDNQ* 23p 254), and the name of the Devil's Nine Stones remained current in the 60s (Wightman 1977 p80).

'A lady from Portland told me in 1965 that her father always used to raise his hat when riding past the stones. They say that the stones are uncountable... A man from Martinstown told me in 1966 that the Winterbourne Abbas stones were the Devil, his wife and childen... I have heard that they were children turned to stone for playing five-stones on a Sunday' (Waring 1977 p32, and as cited in Grinsell 1976 p109).

According to the caption of a photograph of the site taken in 1984, the stones are 'said to have been maidens turned to stone while dancing one Sunday. They are thought by some to 'dance' again at 3.00p.m. (the old noon) on certain days'.

The stones are also known locally (1984) as 'Lady Williams and her Dog', or 'Lady Williams and her Little Dog Fido', in allusion to the family at Bridehead. It is an oddly inconsequential name, reminiscent of the rhyme about Jeffery and Joan at Portesham. Parallels to the other names include a stone circle called the Nine Ladies at Stanton (Derbs.), and another at Harthill in the same county bears the alternative names of the Nine Stones and the Grey Ladies. The several stone circles in Cornwall called the Nine Maidens have been derived from Cornish *maen*, 'stone', but in the light of the English parallels another explanation must be sought.

An informant in 1984 'said an odd thing had happened to him when he went out to look at the site. Taking a view of the stones, he counted them, and there were eight. He thought it was strange, because of the name being Nine, but he counted eight: it was only later that he found there really are nine. Being a folklorist, he knew about countless stone traditions, but had nothing of the sort in mind at the time'.

On the night of 23rd January 1985, there was a peculiar car breakdown at this site. A breakdown van, towing a damaged Ford transit, was passing the stones when its engine cut out and the lights of both vehicles failed. A few minutes later the electric circuits of the vehicles (which were not linked) simultaneously came to life again. At the same time (9.15 p.m.) a similar breakdown occurred on Monkton Hill, when the lights of a Toyota dulled, flashed on and off six or seven times, and then returned to normal. Speculation in the press associated the phenomena with the Eggardon ufo and the more recent sighting of a daylight disc over Rampisham on 19th December, and a connection was implied with the ley *East Lulworth 292*.

Penbury   Hillfort   Pentridge
There was a beacon on Penbury fort (Warne 1872 p252) which was the scene of a bonfire in the 1887 Jubilee and again in the 1897 celebrations; there does not appear to be any mention of it before the 19th century, although the Victorian archaeologists thought it old.

Pilsdon   Hillfort
' 'As much akin as Lewesdon Hill to Pilsdon Pen'. That is, no kin at all. It is spoken of such who have vicinity of habitation or neighbourhood, without the least degree of consanguinity or affinity betwixt them... Yet reader, I assure thee that seamen make the nearest relation betwixt them, calling the one the Cow, the other the Calf; in which forms, it seems, they appear first to their fancies, being eminent sea-marks to such as sail along these coasts' (Fuller 1662 p148).

Other sailors have beens struck with the same fancy at other places: bull, cow, and calf rocks occur along the western coast, most frequently on the north Devon shore. The idea may date back to the Norsemen, who were accustomed to call a larger island the Cow, and its smaller neighbour the Calf: thus we get names like the Calf of Man. Here, as at Eggardon, the needs of sailors promoted building on land: Gerard calls Pilsdon 'a verie high Hill ariseing with a Lodge on the toppe, which serveth for a Marke both by Sea and Lande' (Gerard 1630 p15).

There was a beacon here in 1804.

Portland   Stone coffins; beehive chambers

'When some stone coffins dating from the Roman period were dug up on Portland, they were called the Giant's Graves. The largest sarcophagus measured six feet ten inches, yet I am told of coffins ten feet long – such is the imagined growth-rate of giants. Some stone chambers found in the quarries were called Giants' Beehives (Information from Portland, 1965)' (Waring 1977 p48).

Poundbury   Hillfort   Dorchester (Fordington)

Poundbury has been used for various purposes by Dorchester's authorities and people over the last three centuries. In 1665 the interior of the fort was made to support a plague-house. 'This Company hath agreed with Thomas Tolderville for a plott of grownd at Pombry till Our Lady day next for xx s., and did therevppon give order vnto William Haydon to build an howse thereon for the receiveing of persons to be placed there by Mr. Mayor and the Justices in this time of Contagion'. (Mayo 1908 p537). This may be the watch-house 'built in the tyme of the late siknes' which was ordered to be demolished in 1668, and would explain a crop-mark observed before 1901. 'In a great drought a few years ago the area within Poundbury was searched for signs of destroyed work. Clear witness to the existence of a circular bank around the barrow was seen. The only other mark of old work was about 100 yards south-east of that barrow, where evidently there had been a little rectangular building of about 20ft by 12ft. or so. Very possibly it may have been a shed or small barn' (Moule 1901 p19). This use of the earthworks to contain suspected plague victims implies that the monument was otherwise deserted, so clearly there cannot have been any popular customs involving Poundbury at that date.

In the next century we find that 'in the field, and near this work, the knights of the shire are elected' (Hutchins 1774 1p 575). The elections were held here as usual during the Reform crisis of 1831. in that year there was a crowd of about 12,000 on the hill – about 4,500 of them being franchised – and fighting broke out among the mob, involving Corfe labourers brought in by Calcraft, and the rival factions of Bankes and Erle Drax. The political squibs of each side have allusions to 'yon Booth erected on the rising ground', and the victorious party celebrated in verse;-

'On Pomeroy at the break of day,
The grass was sweet as new-mown hay,
And brightly rose the sixth of May
    On Dorset's Sons of Liberty.

But Pomeroy saw another sight
E're the sun was set at fall of night,
For hot and heady was the fight
    Against the Banksian rabblery...

Few, few shall part where many meet
Without cracked heads or crippled feet,
Too glad to beat a quick retreat
    Before the gallant Yeomanry' (DCM Box File: Politics).

This was the last year when polling was held in the earthworks. There was no other contested election of county M.P.s until 1857, and by then the votes were carried in from nine electoral districts *(DP* 98p 13, 1976).

In 1833-4, 'An Act for better paving, cleansing, lighting... Dorchester' was passed, in consequence of which the sheep fairs were held out of town. Poundbury was chosen as the best new site for the fair, perhaps with the success of Woodbury Hill Fair in mind, and so became the scene of annual festivities. It is possible that there was an earlier annual celebration here: the *DCC* complained, on 24 June 1869, that 'the stupid custom of holding a 'milk fair' on the Poundbury on the first day of the summers' cows being there was kept up on Sunday. It is a matter of surprise that some steps are not instituted to put a stop to this disgraceful desecration of the Lord's Day, when so many roughs get together for the sole purpose of drinking rum and milk'. This custom seems to have become absorbed into the September Sheep Fair; 'Poundbury Fair and local festivities in the past attracted thousands of people to Poundbury and it is within the memory of persons still living, that before the tightening up of the licensing laws, the festivities were often marred by drunken orgies'. The fair itself adhered to traditional conventions: 'In the early days no sales by auction were allowed, sales being effected by personal bargain between buyer and seller' *(DYB* 1942-3 p107). The pattern of feasting was also taken up on Good Friday: 'The older generation remembers the Good Friday jollifications on 'Pummery', when furmity was much in evidence, the chief vendor being an old dame named Trevett, of Grove-buildings. A large barge on the river was, I am told, a 'floating bar'. This observance having become abused by the surreptitious introduction of 'rum and milk' as the popular beverage, it was stopped many years ago, and the licensing laws no doubt expedited its departure' *DCC* 28 March (1935).

At a slightly later date another Dorchester town tradition, that of Bonfire Night, was also transferred to Poundbury. It had for some years been customary for the young men of the town to set fire to a couple of tar-barrels on Guy Fawkes Night, and send them rolling down the incline of the High Street in a more or less destructive fashion while they dressed up as guys, drank a lot and had a good time. On the 5th November 1864 an official placard was put up forbidding the burning of these barrels. 'Eventually one or two tar-barrels were brought out by parties dressed in such grotesque costumes that it would be impossible to speak as to identification, and the police did not appear to have much power in preventing this'. Shortly after, one of the young men was attacked by a constable (who had been burned in effigy the year before) and a great riot broke out; the police retreated into the Town Hall, and the townspeople threw stones at them and tried to break down the doors. Meanwhile the barrels rolled down the High Street as usual. The next year, coercion was tried. The Mayor had handbills posted in the town saying that there would be a bonfire and firework display at Poundbury, and forbidding the celebrations in the streets. 'At eight o'clock in the evening the rifle band, under Mr. Wellspring, marched through the town and, followed by an immense concourse of people, proceeded to the Poundbury where a huge pile of faggots etc. had been built, and which when kindled made a capital bonfire and illumined the neighbourhood around for a great distance'. There were professional and amateur fireworks; some men dressed themselves up as guys with fantastic costumes and faces blackened by burnt cork; and everyone went home by half past ten. The Press observed with a sigh of relief that 'the good old custom can be carried out with such quiet decorum' *(Dorset County Chronicle* 10 Nov 1864; 9 Nov 1865). The innovation of 1865 was close enough to popular ideas for it to be repeated each year, as well as being revived out of season when a Jubilee bonfire was lit here in 1897. In 1886 we read that 'Poundbury is the scene annually of the revels of the Dorchester Bonfire Boys, who on the 5th of November assemble here in their hundreds and, dressed in the most fantastic costumes, indulge in all the enjoyments of the masquerade. The fire is lighted on the tumulus... and forms a fiery landmark for miles around' (Young 1886 p79). As late as

1929 it was still the custom 'to light the Roman rampart up wi' vireworks an' wi' vuzzen on Bonvire night' *(DYB* 1929 p235).

It seems, therefore, that in the 19th century there were feasts or gatherings in Poundbury on at least four annual dates; Good Friday, the last Sunday in June, Fair Day in September, and Guy Fawkes Night. These need not have been contemporary practises, but they seem to have shared each other's characteristics, chiefly drunkenness. The Good Friday gatherings were a local variant of the tradition of ascending hills on certain feastdays: thus games were held at the Hove Barrow in Sussex on Good Friday, and on Palm Sunday there were ascents of Silbury Hill, Martinsell hillfort (Wilts.), and Pontesford hillforts (Salop.). At Silbury it was customary to eat cakes, figs, sugar, and spring water, a sweet diet which may be compared with the furmity prepared at Poundbury. Furmity was eaten elsewhere in Dorset on Good Friday: the practice was kept up at Weymouth into the present century.

The remains of the aqueduct near Poundbury have given rise to speculation. Until the recognition of the monument for what it was, the most obvious stretches were identified as camps, and the terrace just below the hillfort was judged to be the tide-mark of an ancient, lost lake; this seems to have inspired a tradition; 'In its early days a great lake which was fed by the river Frome, lay to the north of the camp. There are stories of monsters which used to inhabit this lake, but no description of them seems to have been attempted. They were just monsters, 'big things with fins' according to one old Dorchester lady' (Collman 1975 p22).

A view of Poundbury in the 1780s, seen from Colliton Walk, from Grose's *Antiquities of England and Wales.*

Powerstock barrow   Round barrow: ? G.3

The excavation of this site is described in a letter from William Sydenham of Wynford Eagle to his uncle, the medical writer: it was written in 1675, and later transcribed by Aubrey (1665-93 p768). Sydenham was persuaded by a visiting relative, 'shee being a grand lover of Antiquities', to set his workmen to barrow-digging: 'on they goe, and when they had cast away the earth it was full of verie great flints, at length wee came to a place perfectly like an Oven curiously clayed round, and in the middest of it a very fayre Urne full of bones very firm and the Urne not rotten, and black ashes a great quantity under the Urne, which is like a butter-pott, made of potters earth, but I must not omitt the chiefest thing that at the first opening this Oven one of my Servants thrust in his hand and pulling it quickly back againe I demanding the reason of him, hee told me it *was very hott*: I did also putt in my hand and it was *warm enough to have baked bread:* several other persons did the like, who can all testifie the truth of it'. The story interested Aubrey, and also Anthony Ettricke, who quotes it in his contribution to the notes on Gibson's Camden. Alas for forteans, Hutchins makes short work of the story: 'I was informed in 1741, by the Rev. Mr. Birket, rector of West-Compton, that several people then living had assured him, that what related to the oven and the heat in it, was an invention of one Paul Salisbury, who was employed in this work, in order to please Mr. Sydenham, pick his pocket, and divert himself by laughing at him for recording it in a great book'. In later years Salisbury 'declared in all company, that this story was invented by him...Mr. Sydenham was a weak man, and easily imposed upon; and Salisbury an arch, impudent, lying fellow' (Hutchins 1774 1p 527).

In locating this barrow at Powerstock, I have followed Legg's notes on Aubrey, rather than Grinsell, who places it in Wynford Eagle.

Puckysbarry   ? Barrow   Winfrith Newburgh

A document of 1451 mentions *Puckysbarry* and *Puckysway* in this parish, 'barrow and way of the *puca* or goblin'.

Rainbarrows   Round barrows: G. 22-4   Puddletown

The custom of lighting a bonfire at this site on Guy Fawkes night provides the framework for the third chapter of *The Return of the Native*. The fire was composed of furze faggots, forming 'a pyramid of furze thirty feet in circumference' on top of one barrow. The novelist describes the associated festivities, with snatches of song, gossip, and dancing in the embers. The site was evidently selected for its unparalleled view of the land to the south, across the Frome valley and the waste beyond as fas as the hills that rise next to the sea.

The use of the site for a beacon is described by the name author in *The Dynasts* II. v, where the Rainbarrows are 'three tumuli. On the sheltered side of the most prominent of these stands a hut of turves with a brick chimney. In front are two ricks of fuel, one of heather and furze for quick ignition, the other of wood, for slow burning'. The beaconkeepers discuss their duty, which is 'whenever you see Kingsbere-Hill Beacon fired to the eastward, or Black' on to the westward, light up; and keep your second fire burning for two hours'. See Blackdown and Woodbury in this Inventory.

There appears to have been a long tradition of hill-top fires in this parish. *Beldene* occurs as a fieldname in 1383, and *Belbury* in 1579, both names containing *bel*, 'fire, pyre', and meaning the hill or barrow of the fires. The site is not located by Mills, but may be near the modern Bellbury Close, 758. 943. The beacon on Beacon Hill (so called on the

1811 OS) is first mentioned in 1625 as *le becon apud Whiteborne;* it lies on a hill north-east of the Rainbarrows. Presumably the name commemorates an earlier site than that chosen in 1804.

Rampisham   Roman pavement
In 1799 this was discovered on common land, and a sketch made of it. Immediately after the drawing was made, it was broken up by the ignorant neighbours, who supposed that some treasure was concealed under it' (Hutchins 1861-70 2p 693).

Rawlesbury   Hillfort   Hilton/Stoke Wake
A great wooden cross, set into a circular stone base, stands on a commanding position by the eastern entrance of the fort. It is about twelve feet high, made of two rough boughs strapped together with wire, and was put up in 1966 – a comparatively late date for the Christianisation of a prehistoric site (Gant 1980 p83).
The monument is the scene of an annual religious festival: 'One Sunday each summer the ancient hillfort becomes as busy as a town on market day... In view of the cross, a sermon is read and hymns are sung in this outdoor service for people of all denominations' *(Western Gazette* 25 March 1983).

Rempstone stone circle   Corfe Castle
'The Agglestone rock at Studland is reputed to have been thrown by the Devil from the Isle of Wight, at Corfe Castle, but fell short by five miles or so. There are also some small stones at Rempstone, halfway between Studland and Corfe Castle, which are also supposed to have been aimed at the castle' (Palmer 1973 p106).
This is one of a large group of variants which have developed around the story that the Devil threw a natural monument, the Agglestone, from the Needles towards Corfe Castle. He is variously said to have been aiming at the Castle, at Sherborne or Bindon Abbies, or at Salisbury Cathedral; and some minor sarsens in the line of flight are attributed to him as well as the Agglestone. The tradition about Rempstone is obviously modern, since the site was not discovered until this century.

Robin Hood's Butts   Round barrows: G. 2-8   Verwood
'The tumuli in this neighbourhood (Pistle Down) are called by the peasantry, 'Robin Hood's Butts' '(Wake Smart, quoted by Warne, 1866 ii p27).
The name is also applied to barrows in Shropshire, Staffordshire, Somerset, and Yorkshire. The comparison with the raised earthen butts used in archery practice must date the phrase to the Middle Ages.

Rowbarrow   ? Barrow   Corfe Castle
The Hundred of Rowbarrow is first mentioned (as *Rugebergahundredum)* in 1183. 'Near *Tapers Hill,* and south of it, is a lane called *Rowbarrow Lane,* and in a ground near it, the hundred court was formerly held' (Hutchins 1774 1p 213). These places lie near Woolgarston, and the meeting-place would have been at about 983809. Its name ('rough barrow') is one of the commonest that are given to tumuli.

Seven Ditches   IA village site   Gussage St. Michael
An alternative, and probably obsolete, name for the site known as Gussage Cow Down. It first appears in a Sixpenny Handley charter of 956 *(DP* 58p 117, 1936) as *Seven Diche,*

the name being applied to the westernmost of the earthworks, along which runs the boundary between Gussage St. Michael and Sixpenny Handley. The obvious interpretation would be that of the later traditions, that seven ditches were seen or imagined on the site: but Grundy is inclined to derive the name from a mythical Sevenna. He observes that Ackling Dyke, which runs near this boundary, 'is called *Seuene Strete* in a South Damerham charter', and suggests that the hypothetical Sevenna 'may be one of those female names like Icenilde and Buggilde which are applied to other Roman roads'. Some such convention in the Middle Ages is suggested by the use of the name Maiden Way in Westmoreland, and the name *Sarn Elen,* 'Helena's Causeway', for Roman roads in Wales, following the account in the *Dream of Maxen Wledig.* But the existence of the later forms at Gussage is a strong argument against such a meaning here. In 1613 the parish register of Cranborne records the burial of 'a woman wch dyed in the snowe at Sevenditches' (Hutchins 1861-70 3p 396), and later Aubrey wrote 'Mem. the *Seaven ditches,* between Woodyates and Blandford... I cannot find any Account of them. The Rode from Salisbury to Blandford goes through them: they lie upon the line, the sayd line being the seaventh ditch' (1665-93 p908). The name was still current in 1887, when Wake Smart ascribes it to 'several British trackways ascending the hill in close contiguity... A cross section would give that number of banks with their intervening ditches. From time immemorial the peasantry of the district have known it by that name' *(Arch. Journal* 44p 380). The site is complex enough for any number of ditches to be discerned, and the count of seven is simply another assimilation to a conventional number.

At Gussage Hill, another name for the area, a bonfire was lit in 1897.

Shipton Hill   Hillfort   Shipton Gorge
There may be a beacon shown here on the map of 1539, but its geography is confused. The hill is called Shipton Beacon on Taylor's map of 1765 and the O.S. of 1811; the beacon was used in the scare of 1804 – 'furze faggots were used to fuel the fire and sufficient had to be provided to burn for two hours. Richard Roberts, of Burton, was responsible for paying the rent for the Shipton beacon of 7/- per annum' (Gale 1983 p83).

The two carved stone heads found in Shipton in 1958 and dated on stylistic grounds to the Iron Age may have come from this site. They had been buried in a bank close to the village, and it is possible that they were deposited there in mediaeval or modern times as a structural talisman, a thing to bring good luck.

Sixpenny Handley   Roman hoard
'Herb Lucas' father once saw a man in armour riding on a white horse near a large oak tree by the junction of the Newtown and Deneland road. Other people are said to have seen this apparition also. A hoard of Roman coins, probably that recorded by General Pitt-Rivers in *Excavations in Cranborne Chase,* was found in the allotment on which the oak tree stood, and the horseman has not been seen since. The villagers think he was the guardian of the coins' (Parke 1963 p483: story collected 1939-41).

Slaughter Barrow   Long barrow: G.I.   Gillingham
'Tradition states that it was the burial place of those who were slain in a battle between the Saxons and the Danes... The blood shed on this occasion flowed as far as a place still called Slaughter Gate, and which is distant about a quarter of a mile from the barrow' *(Notes and Queries* 1 ser. 12p 364, 1855).

This battle is identified by the contributor with the battle of Peonna of 1016. The legend may be an embroidered form of antiquarian speculation on the placename. The modern form of the legends speaks of a battle between Alfred and the Danes; in Wavering Lane the Danish army *wavered,* and at last *peace* was made in Peasemarsh (Howe 1983 p18).

Spetisbury   Hillfort
The fort appears to have been the site of a hill-top fair in the 10th century. Three Saxon pennies were found 'when the ring was prepared for sowing' in about 1780; they were of the reign of Edgar, minted by Wynstan; of Edward the Martyr, minted by Wulfgar; and of Ethelred II. W.G. Maton, who sent a sketch of the first two coins to Gough (Hutchins 1796-1814 3p 136; not illustrated in the third edition) identified their mints as Towcester in Northamptonshire and Stamford, which would suggest that trade was coming in over a considerable distance.

'The old natives of Spetisbury will tell you that before ever Blandford was built, there on the downs between Spetisbury and Charlton, stood the City of Bland, and that you can see to this day the shape of its streets marked on the Downs... An old Spetisbury farmer says there was once a prison camp for French solidiers during the Napoleonic Wars on the site of the ancient city and he adds, 'They d'zay that when the people where diggin' out an' makin' up Badbury Rings and Castle Rings there were only one pick an' shovel between 'em, zoo they did pass the tools back an' for'ard, when oone were pickin' tother were shovellin' ' (Knott 1976 p175).

These stories of lost grandeur are often found in communities which have seen an urban neighbour grow in prominence. In the 1630s, Stoborough was 'scarce worth a Remembring... but the Inhabitants beleeve, that *ab initio non fuit sic;* for they are not ashamed to affirme, the Village to be much more ancient then Warham, and will tell you many faire Traditions for it' (Gerard p55); again, at Shaftesbury 'the inhabitants have a tradition, that an old City stood upon the place which is call'd the Castle Green, and by some Bolt-bury, now a fair plain' (Camden col. 48 n17, Gibson's note). It is said of Dunditch field, the site of the deserted mediaeval village of Bardolfeston (in Puddletown), that 'Dunditch was a thriving town/When London was a vuzzey down' *(Dorset Countryside* 1p 57, 1976). And Poole makes the claim: 'Poole was a thriving town/When Liverpool was a furzy down' (Palmer 1973 p20). The closest parallel to the city of Bland comes from the Somerset-Devon border, where a lost city called Ford is supposed to have stretched over the Blackdown Hills (Matthews 1923 p26).

Such stories are interesting for the insight they give into popular ideas of archaeology and landscape history. A similar kind of folk geology is implied by another informant: 'There is a legend that the hill, known as Spetisbury, but to me Castle Rings, and Badbury Rings, were at one time cliffs and the sea came as a bay thus far inland' *(Dorset* 7p 28, 1968).

The building of monuments with only a single pick and shovel, or some such variant, is a story often told of giants. The motif occurs in the Irish *Dinnschenchas,* and therefore dates to at least the 12th century in the British Isles. We read of 'Femen and Fera, two brothers... One billhook and one shovel of iron between the two. When Femen was shovelling, Fera was hacking. And each of them used to fling his billhook and his shovel in his proper turn to the other over the plain into Rae Urchair ('Field of a Cast'). Hence 'Mag Femin', and 'Mag Fera' *'(Folk-lore* 4, 1893). A longer version of the story comes from Shropshire, where two giant brothers, living on View Edge and Norton Camp on each side of Stokesay, kept their treasure under Stokesay Castle; they threw the key back and forth as occasion required. One day it was lost, and the treasure remains in the castle vault, guarded by a great raven (Burne 1883 p7, 11. She cites several German parallels). And there were two industrious giants in Scotland who threw their shoe-making tools to and fro across the Dornoch Firth.

Studland barrow
Round barrow: G.9

'In 1892 a granite obelisk was erected on the site of this barrow by George Burt, to commemorate his introduction of a new water supply to Swanage. A few years later it fell down and had to be re-erected. In the second world war it collapsed a second time' (Calkin 1986 p11). This obelisk has now passed into the hands of the National Trust.

Sturminster Newton Castle
Hillfort, with mediaeval structure superimposed

King Alfred lived here, according to a local tradition passed on by Olive Knott *(DYB* 1963-4p 124). 'Curious tales are told of it by old people that for nearly a hundred years have passed away. They told of a well near the ruins, where valuable silver articles are buried, perhaps some future day a search may be made' (DRO: MR44p 41) Others said it was a golden table that was hidden in the well *(DP* 24 p. lxxvii 1903). The earlier reference is part of the reminiscences of Robin Young, a Sturminster man looking back to his schooldays in the 1820s. Elsewhere he states that teachers should 'not allow absurd stories to be told before timid and sensitive children. A case in point – a story was often told them of a wild and savage Cat which haunted the remains of the old castle and was often seen on Newton hill. Such horrid tales were told of this monster cat, with eyes as big as tea saucers, that many children were afraid to pass that way, and not only children but grown-up people would be so afraid that they would walk on the main road below the hill to avoid the creature. I am pleased to know that foolish tale is quite forgotton'.

In a more recent source, the legend is of 'a 'terrifying creature' which ran along a track parallel to the main road at a place called the Hollow, near the old castle at Newton. A local clergyman knew someone who spoke of it as a dog in 1965' (Waring 1977 p9). As Waring notes, there was a query in an early number of *SDNQ* (10p 120, 1906) about the legend of a 'Shillingstone Castle Cat'. This presumably haunted the moated site at Bere Marsh *(le Castel* in 1546). At Friar Waddon in Portesham there were warnings of 'a large black cat with staring eyes and a luminous tail' (Waring p4). More recently (about 1975) a phantom black cat with glowing eyes was seen by a girl in the suburbs of Wyke Regis. These accounts are interesting, as they form a link between the the phantom black dogs of conventional folklore (for which Waring's first chapter and his earlier article in *DP* provide the best set of data) and the modern quasi-zoological apparitions of great wild cats in Britain, of which the Surrey puma was the first notable case, and the Beast of Exmoor the most recent; a survey of sightings of the Bournemouth puma is currently in progress. It is as if the great cat apparitions formed a secondary class of ghosts which only began to thrive after the eclipse of black dog traditions; one thinks of the parallel the conflict of red and grey squirrels.

Thickthorn barrow
Long barrow: G. II   Gussage St. Michael

'I was informed by Prof. Piggott that when this long barrow was opened in 1933, the excavators were constantly asked by the local people whether they were looking for, or had found, the golden or silver coffin said to be buried there' (Grinsell 1959 p56).

Thorncombe Beacon
? Barrow: ? G. 2   Symondsbury

'Some mounds on Thorncombe Beacon and Langdon Hill are called the Devil's Jumps'

(Waring 1977 p57). The site at Thorncombe Beacon may be a barrow, although the mounds at Langdon (in Chideock) are natural. Traditions of the Devil's Jumps are fairly widespread in West Dorset, places being so identified at Marshwood, Thorncombe, and Bridport: in the most coherent version, the Devil was kicked by the Abbot of Forde, and bounced south towards the sea. (For one version, see *SDNQ* 21p 69).

A beacon appears here on the map of 1539. It is Thorncombe Beacon on the 1811 O.S., and was used for a bonfire in 1897; this is probably the beacon photographed in the *DYB* for 1915, p36 – a stack of turves on a cliff edge, to be fired when the Germans came.

Thursdyche ? Entrenchment Preston
'Ditch haunted by a *thyrs* or ogre.' The *fossat' apud Thursdyche* are referred to in 15th-century documents (1451, 1461, and 1475), but cannot be located at a modern site, unless they refer to Preston Roman villa. The same name appears as Thursditch in Kempsford (Glos.) in 1801. The thurse, which is first mentioned in *Beowulf,* was a kind of demonic giant: the parallel with Lancashire names like thurse-hole suggests that the Preston name implies a haunting, rather than 'ditch dug by a thurse'.

Tinkers Barrow Round barrow: G.1 Owermoigne
So called by the O.S. (1888). The name suggests that here, as at Culliford Tree, there was a recognised gipsy meeting-place.

Toten berg R-B village site Farnham
'Look-out station': the site is mentioned in the Sixpenny Handley charter of 956. Grundy identifies it as 'probably the earthern enclosure at the side of the British village, nearly ¾ mile north of Farnham'at 960.161. This, like the Ward- names, would belong to an earlier beacon tradition that did not involve fires.

Upwey barrows Unlocated: G. 21a
In his diary entry for 2nd October 1621, William Whiteway of Dorchester records the visit of two treasure-hunters here. 'This day came certain commissioners with the broad seal of England to dig in a hill at Upway near Dorchester for some treasure that lies hidden underground, but having spend three days about it, they went away having found nothing but a few bones, saying they meant to dig at Bincombe and under that pretence went away'. *(DP* 13, 1892).

Grinsell has tracked down the original 'Special Commission to Rich. Ryves and others to dig for treasure supposed to be in certain parts of a down in the parish of Upwey', which was issued only eight days before the men arrived in Dorset. He notes that 'such authorisations tended to be issued in areas where treasure had already been found, perhaps by illicit digging' (Grinsell 1982 p12).

The Verne Hillfort Portland
Two beacons are shown in this part of the island on the map of 1539. The Tithe Map of 1841 shows the earthworks of the Verne as they were before the Prison was built there: and at the south-west corner is a round enclosure against the line of the rampart. This may have been the beacon-hearth, although the similarity to the site at Abbotsbury should induce caution. The same map shows a signal-station just north of the fort, and both a beacon and a signal-station are marked on the 1804 map.

'It was the Verne Signal which in may, 1804, during thick sea fog, gave a false alarm and started the rumour that the French had landed on the Island. This created a tremendous panic throughout Dorset, and led to grave fears for the safety of George III who was at that time paying one of his visits to Weymouth' (Bettey 1970 p103).

The hillfort is assumed to have been destroyed when the modern fort, now the prison, was built on the site, but this may not be altogether true. Although the southern ramparts and ditches of the Victorian defenses are smooth-laid turf, there are banks to the north and east which have a much rougher outline and more ragged vegetation. They may have been taken over directly from the prehistoric earthworks.

The obelisk in Weatherbury Rings, and the plantation which has grown up around it: from Charles Harper's *The Hardy Country,* 1904.

Wardstone Barrow Round barrow: G. 19 Chaldon Herring

The site is so named by the O.S. (1811). It lies on a high part of Chaldon Down overlooking the coast, and must be another of the Ward-placenames. Beacons are marked nearby on the modern map. The word 'stone' suggests that there was a stone on top of the mound here: it may have marked the spot out for the hoblers.

Weatherby Castle Hillfort Milborne St. Andrew

Hutchins (1774 1p 44) refers to 'an obelisk lately erected' within this monument by Edmund Morton Pleydell, who acquired the estate in 1728. The obelisk still stands among the trees of a plantation, from which it is hardly distinguishable until a close view: it consists of a grey plinth about ten feet high, supporting some sixty feet of tapering red brick, topped by a corroded metal sphere. There is no inscription; two of its sides are green with ivy, and the brickwork is falling from decay.

Werybarowe ? Barrow Canford Magna

The site is first mentioned as *Wyreberge* in 1275, when it is said to be in the 'launds of Caneford': these would be the Lawns, 'a large tract of heathy ground', which Hutchins locates near the mines at Parkstone.

'A commission despatched in 1462 to William White, Mayor of Poole, speaks of 'setting the accustomed watches of Wurebarowe by Pole, for the safety of the town and the adjacent county' '(Smith 1951 2p 46). And in 'an old manuscript' (now lost) of Poole Corporation, dated 1544, 'is a list of 'all ther namys that of owlde tyme have been accustomyd and owght to fynd hoblers to kepe the watche, in the tyme of warre, at the bekon callyd Werybarowe'. After this follow lists of the hoblers who kept watch, &c., in the years 1513, 1540, 1543, and 1544' (Sydenham 1839 p98).

The Henrican map shows three beacons by Poole (the Corporation were taking no chances), and White's analysis of the area is good enought for *Werybarowe* to be identified as the middle beacon, although he was ignorant of the placename and followed Sydenham in locating the 1462 reference at Worbarrow Tout.

Whitcombe barrow Round barrow: G. 6

An informant in 1983 described the singing of this barrow. According to my notes taken at the time, 'About nine or ten years ago he had gone to see the Culliford Tree barrow group. Looking north from the point where a minor road turns off the main one, you can see Culliford Tree, with the tree clump on it, to your left, and to your right a smaller barrow, the first of a cemetery extending off in that direction. From this smaller barrow he, and a friend with him, heard a sound which they identified as the traditional singing. It was a humming, whining noise: when pressed for a description, he said it was like the sound of a jet engine, but soft and far off. It did not come from any point in the barrow, but seemed to be pervasive in the area around the site. He had never heard the sound at that place, before or since'.

Wild Church Bottom Round barrows: G. 1-8 Verwood

The area was known as Wild Church Valley in 1865, according to J.H. Austen *(Archaeological Journal* 14p 107) who thought it might owe its name to Protestants meeting secretly on Boveridge Heath at the time of the Marian persecution. There are several barrows around the bottom, including Grinsell's Verwood 1 which is called, or stands on a hill which is called, Stephen's Castle; one of these may be the eponymous Wild Church. Hutchins (1861-70 3p 388) and the 1887 O.S. use the name Wild Church

Bottom; on the latter we find that Mount Ararat lies to the north-east of the valley and a Wesleyan Methodist Chapel to the south-west. Doubtless both names, like Church Barrow in Handley, commemmorates the meeting-place of Methodists who had found their ark of salvation on a Dorset Ararat.

Wilkswood   R-B settlement   Langton Matravers

'What of the green fairies seen at Wilkswood in their Phrygian hats?' asks John Cox in the *Dorset Evening Echo,* July 1977. He seems to identify them as 'ghosts of bygone Romans, who camped in these parts, busy in forage caps about some routine task'. I have been unable to get further information, but the apparition is presumably connected with the R-B settlements in the area. In 1944, J.B. Calkin found Samian sherds and a dolphin brooch at Wilkswood (Calkin 1968 p24).

In the same wood 'the ghost of a walled-in nun is said to appear around the foundations of a religious house and a pot of gold and the usual coffin are said to be waiting for a finder' (Benfield 1950 p85). The coffin would be better suited to the Roman remains than the mediaeval ones.

Wimborne St. Giles: the battle barrows   Round barrows: G. 64-7

'The four barrows north of the Park were stated, by a local farmer to LVG about 1934, to have 'probably covered the bones of some Roman warriors killed in a battle' (Grinsell 1959). In a similar vein is 'The tradition, told to me by several people, that Boadicea, Queen of the Iceni, fought a battle at Handley Cross', which 'probably originated because of the large number of barrows in the area, which tradition claims to be the war cemetery for the dead from the battle' (Parke p483; material collected 1939-41). These traditions are the fossils of an outdated archaeology. In the 17th century Aubrey attempted to identify the sites of the battles mentioned by classical authors through the observation of barrow groups; three centuries later, the discarded assumption has become part of folklore.

Wimborne St. Giles: the fairy barrows   Round barrows: G. 31-6

'I was told one evening a man lay down to rest on top of one of the barrows on Bottlebush Down, and was astonished to see a crowd of little people in leather jerkins, who came and danced round him. Since hearing this tale, I have been told that the man was the late curate of Handley, the Rev. A.R.T. Bruce, but unfortunately he died before I could confirm this' (Parke 1963 p482).

Windmill Barrow   Round barrow: G. 1   Lytchett Matravers

A story about this site is recorded by F. Carré in her typescript *Notes on the Story of Lytchett Matravers,* compiled in 1927. Carre1 lived from 1852 to the 1950s, and this story, like much of her folklore, is derived from a Miss Blaney, so it is probably of Victorian date.

Formerly the road which runs over the hill, east of Windmill Barrow, carried traffic to Blandford. 'Many years ago a carter was taking corn along this road with some heavy cart horses in the very early hours of the morning. All at once the animals refused to budge, answer to rein or whip they would not. The man got off the wagon to ascertain the reason and found a sort of shapeless mass in the horse's way, which he summoned courage to remove to the side of the road and could not by any means account for it. He got the animals past with difficulty and on the return journey they simply got out of hand and ran away when they came to the place again. I heard long afterwards some human bones had been dug up near the precise spot where this occurred'.

The association of a haunted barrow with a later discovery of bones has been described at Ashmore in this Inventory. There is a very similar story from Somerset: a track near Creech Hill in Bruton was haunted until two bodies were found during quarrying in the 1880s. The haunt took the form of a formless clutching black shape (Tongue 1967 p121). Another shapeless apparition like that at Windmill Barrow is reported from the Minehead-Bridgewater road: 'a white summat... It were alive – kind of woolly like a cloud or a wet sheep – and it slid up and all over him' (Briggs 1977 p33).

Winterborne Came barrow   Round barrow

A phantom army was heard by F. Carré, in the late summer of 1918, at a barrow on Came Down gold course – probably the one at 688.869, which is one the O.S. but not in Grinsell. According to her account *(The Singing Barrow,,* in *DYB* 1936 p149), she set out from Upwey Halt, in a mood of depression, and wandered over the golf links and the downs until she came to a piece of high ground with an extensive view, and sat down on a small barrow. 'I sat dreaming, looking over the downs, when I became conscious of voices singing far away, and with a certain rhythm – 'Soldiers singing', I said to myself. Hundreds of soldiers passed my house on the High Road, day and night, and very often sang as they marched. So I listened dreamily, not paying much real heed. I became aware gradually that the singing was coming nearer – it seems to consist of a sort of glad sonorous chant. Long sentences, beginning in low tones, rising to a higher note, and ending with a sort of glad chant and a crash of steel or iron against steel or iron, on it came, louder and nearer. It was grand, triumphant! Suddenly I jumped to my feet again quite consicous of where I was. 'Why! It is Latin they are singing' I exclaimed aloud, and all was dead silence instantly. I was quite alone, miles from any road, not a soldier in sight, not a possibility of any soldiers within hearing'.

Carré does not identify the site, but having followed her account on the ground, I feel fairly sure that the barrow is one of those at the north end of the golf course. Enquiries at the Golf Club, however, failed to reveal any knowledge of the story.

Winterborne Houghton barrow   Round barrow: ? one of G. 7-9

A barrow here was the scene of a curious treasure-seeking incident a few years ago. The publication of Kit Williams' book *Masquerade,* with its artful and artistic clues to the whereabouts of a golden hare buried somewhere in England, set many otherwise sane people off on the trail of buried treasure. It was assumed by several readers that the gold would lie at a prehistoric site, Stonehenge and Brent Knoll being two favourites: a similar idea inspired a couple from Sussex (Gascoigne 1984 p149). Through various calculations and inspirations, they concluded that the hare lay at 802.013 (Milton Abbas), at 725 ft. above sea level, on crown property. A small group of tumuli were at this height in the neighbourhood, and just before Christmas 1980 the couple visited the site and found further apparent confirmations: a rectangular enclosure of barbed wire, for instance, which brought to mind that *Masquerade* is an anagram of *Made Square.* Masqueraders were fond of this sort of thing. On a later visit 'they came face to face with a man carrying a shotgun and a game bag. They asked if the tumuli were on public ground and he confirmed that they were. But while they were digging in their chosen area (to one side of the tumuli), a small lady in a peaked cap came striding up. She announced herself as Mrs. Brown and asked what they were doing. They replied that they were an archaeological team from Exeter University investigating the problem of subsidence in tumuli. She protested that this was her own private land'. The earlier informant had been, as Gascoigne puts it, 'the local poacher, a man committed by his trade to the proposition that all land is public'. The advent of Mrs. Brown seems to have put an end to the treasure-hunting, and the couple were following another set of clues when, two years later, the golden hare was found by some more hard-headed researchers.

Winterborne Kingston — Roman coffin

A leaden coffin was found, a few years before 1850, 'in a field on the left border of the road to Bere... The village people say it was the body of 'one of the kings'; and it is curious that, previously to the discovery, a tradition lingered amongs them that a 'golden coffin' was buried somewhere in the parish' (Hutchins 1861-70 1p 149).

Witchampton — Roman vase

'A Roman vase recently found at Witchampton' was shown as a new acquisition of the County Museum in 1934. 'Mrs. McGeagh explained the remarkable circumstances in which this interesting find was made. 'About six weeks ago' she said, 'my friend who does all the digging for me (Mr. Frank Bevan) dreamt there was a box of gold in his garden at a certain place'. Continuing, she told how he went to the spot and dug and found this beautifully ornamented and marvellously well–preserved vase' *(DP 56P. xxviii)*.

Woodbury Hill — Hillfort — Bere Regis

'Woodberrie Hill,' we learn from an estate survey of 1617, 'is a place nere to the towne of Beere which hath in time beene a stronge and steepe forte or an intrenchment for souldiers upon which hill is yearlie a very great fayre kepte upon the topp and middle' (DRO: Photo 248/11–12). It was also the site of a mediaeval chapel, and both chapel and fair became part of Dorset folklore.

The chapel is first mentioned as the *capelle de Wodebury* in 1408, but if Mills is right in identifying it with the *capellam de Bere* in 1205, it may be of 12th-century foundation, and contemporary with the hill-top chapels of Milton Abbas, Christchurch, and Winchester. In 1405 we hear of 'John Sperhauk, chaplain of Wodebury', and the same post was held by John Luyde in 1412; in 1408 the 'walls, doors, windows, roof and timber-work of Wodebury chapel are defective through the Rector's fault' (Chandler 1984 p3, 73, 107). The site appears to have had a patron well, marked Anchoret's Well on the O.S., and first mentioned by Hutchins. 'A tradition exists of a deep well, called the 'Anchoret's Well' on the hill, in which is supposed to be a valuable treasure in some such form as a golden table or tablet. To this well, it is said, people used to flock on the 21st of September, to drink of the water, many virtues being attributed to it. Money offerings were made on the occasion, and were paid over to the Abbess of Tarrant. A deep well of never-failing water still exists on the Hill, but it is not now used, and is, by some, thought not to be the ancient Anchorets Well. Also somewhere, on the western side of the Hill, it is said, are the foundations of a church, dedicated to 'Saint Anchoretta' and which was in reality the mother church of that of St. John the Baptist, Bere Regis' (Pickard-Cambridge 1885). The hill was called 'Woodbury St. Mary' by Bere people, and the fair was originally (as we know from a reference of 1282) held on the Nativity of the Blessed Virgin; so, as Pickard-Cambridge argues, the chapel must have been dedicated to her. The foundations were seen by Hutchins, who says, 'On the west side of this hill was a chantry or chapel, whose foundations are still visible' (1774 1p39); but they are now obscured. The group of religious customs here, comprising an annual feast, a visit to the patron saint's well, a fair, and the making of offerings at a geomantically sited chapel, is unusual in Wessex, but much resembles the gatherings that have taken place in Catholic Ireland up to modern times. Something similar appears to have been done at Milton Abbas, where the girls of the village would meet at St. Catherine's Well, on the feast of that saint, and proceed to St. Catherines's Chapel on the hill-top, within its mediaeval earthwork (Hope 1893 p32. But his evidence is flawed by a confusion between Milton and Abbotsbury).

Woodbury Hill Fair was held on the authority of charters of 1232, 1236 and 1267 (Hutchins 1861-70 1p135), although the existence of an earlier trading centre in the area is indicated by the finding of a silver penny of Offa (757-796) and a silver denier of Pepin (751-768) by the Roman road north of Roke farm *(DP* 195p151,1983). The fair may have been established at the hill because there was a chapel of an anchorite there: for something like this did happen later, under Henry VII, at Southampton. A hermit called William Geoffrey was given the privilege of a fair on Holy Trinity and the next three days. 'This fair was held around the hermitage, and the profits arising therefrom belonged partly to the hermit and partly to the town' (Shor 1892 p135).

The folk view of the origin of the Fair is given by a tradition from the Munuel family of Bloxworth. 'A pedlar, travelling with a pack of cloth at his back, was over-taken in a great storm, and thoroughly soaked, pack and all, with the rain. Passing over the Hill as the storm ceased and the sun shone out, he unpacked and spread the cloth out to dry; the country people living near, struck with the goodness of the cloth, then and there made such advantageous offers for it, that in a few hours the whole was disposed of, to the satisfaction of all parties. The tradition continues that at about the same time the following year the Pedlar again passed that way, and this time unpacked his goods purposely to invite purchasers, and with such success that he was induced to repeat it in following years: other traders also joined with goods of other descriptions, until at length the business was still more enlarged and a charter obtained' (Pickard-Cambridge 1885).

In 1242 the incumbent of the church at Bere was entitiled to 'all offerings made on the feast of the Nativity of the Blessed Virgin Mary at Woodbury' (VCH Dorset 2p13). The fair was evidently of some importance in the 13th century. We learn from the building accounts for Corfe Castle that when in 1282, the news of an unexpected visit from the King had stirred his workmen into extra labour, they had to buy ironwork at the Fair – nails and locks and keys (Hutchins 1861-70 1p493). This is not the kind of thing stocked by casual pedlars. Livestock was also being sold, for the customary of Winterborne Stickland manor, set down in 1334, obliges some of the tenants to drive their lord's cattle to five markets including Woodbury (Hutchins 1861-70 1p331). It appears that administrative business was also carried out at the Fair. In 1315-16 two land-owners, Joan de Vivonia and Henry de Mortimer, held small fractions of the manor of Sturminster Marshall by a service which included 'finding a tything-man for Sturminster Marshall, at the sheriff's turn, at Woodborough, twice a year' (Hutchins 1861-70 3p338, 341). Sturminster lay in Cogdean Hundred, so that in the ordinary course of things the tithingmen should have met at Cogdean Elms; presumably the annual fair was a more convenient rendezvous for the sheriff.

According to 13th-century confirmations of the liberties of Tarrant Abbey, the Abbess was to receive part of the tolls from the Fair (Hutchins 1861-70 3p121). The other part was claimed by lay landowners; after the Reformation the whole profit went to the Turbervilles. 'Woodbery Hill with the profits of the fair there' was the subject of litigation in 1595 (DCM: Dorset Suits 5p95) and in 1693 *(SDNQ* 21p333).

The fair continued to have an economic influence throughout Dorset and beyond. In 1648 the Dorchester records show that most of the town was supposed to be absent on

Woodbury Fair Eve (Mayo 1908 p618)., and a Dorchester woman's lawsuit over ten shillings 'lent at Woodbery Hill faire' in 1674 (DCM: Dorset Suits 4p99) is witness to the attendance of townspeople there. In 1687 Aubrey reckoned it one of the most considerable fairs in Wessex (Aubrey 1687 p108). Its importance to Dorset people is shown by the way in which widely dispersed communities speak of the fair day when they mean the 8th or 18th of September. It is a recognised date in places as far apart as Piddletrenthide and Wyke Regis in the 17th century *(SDNQ* 30p203, 1976; *DP* 102p3, 1980); the Quarter Sessions order books for Dorset, 1625-37, speak of Woodbury Day *(DP* 99p1,1977); at Hampreston in 1649 it is Woodberrie Tyde *(SDNQ* 19p152,1928); Woodbury Fair at Hooke, and Woodbury Fair Day at Evershot, in 1774 (Hutchins 1774 1p294, 504); Woodbury Tide at Chideock in 1796 (Hutchins 1796-1814 1p549); while at Lytchett Minster in the late 19th century it was still a customary date. 'Fires were commenced on the day following Woodbury Hill Fair, no matter the temperature' (DYB 1962-3p99).

In Hutchins' time the fair attracted traders from Birmingham, Bristol, Exeter, London, and Norwich, and was still one of the greatest in southern England, although he regards it as being in decline: 'Vast quantities of hops, cloth, cheese and almost all commodities, were sold here; on the first day by wholesale, on the rest by retail. Here was also a fair for horses every day. The tolls formerly amounted to £100 clear; but have much decreased since 1730 and have of late years been very inconsiderable, not amounting to more than £30 or £40 a year'. An 1803 book of fairs repeats this description, and *Owen's New Book of Fairs* in 1824 says, 'Sept. 18, and five following days, for all sorts of cattle, horses, hops, cheese cloth, haberdashery, and all sorts of goods'.

Originallly held on Septemeber 8th, the Nativity, the fair was moved forward 10 days at the 1753 alteration of the calendar, as were others such as Weyhill and Yarnbury, and was held on the five days after Sept. 18th. By 1885 it had been shortened to two days, 21 and 22 Sept., but was continuing to shrink: in 1906 the sale of sheep was discontinued, and by 1938 the fair consisted only of entertainments. It was discontinued during the War, and a revival after 1945 was unsuccessful.

There is a delightful piece of Augustan occasional verse by David Okeden (DRO: D545/F8) in which he describes a trip to the Fair in 1796. The visiting gentry are surrounded by a mob of life –

> 'Men, Women, Carts, Coaches, Pigs, Wheel-barrows, Cattle,
> Gowns, Petticoats, Bonnets, all such sorts of gear,
> Gin, Cyder, Rum, Brandy, Ale, Dorchester Beer,'

but their main interests are in the fairground entertainments. There is a wild-beast show, where 'a Keeper savage as the Beasts he feeds' stands, shouting 'Walk in, walk in!' at the entrance of a tent decorated with lively paintings of the elephants, tigers and leopards concealed inside. Here a beggar pleads for charity, and there a stall sells gingerbread, cakes, and pies. The gingerbread, after the old fashion, is made in human shape and then painted and gilded to look like a king. 'How many Monarchs,' thinks the poet,

> 'gay with golden robes
> Some swaying sceptres, and some grasping globes
> Are doom'd at sad reverse of fate severe
> To cloy the stomach of some new breach'd dear'.

New breach'd' because it was the custom for boys to put on their first pair of trousers at the Fair. The cookery stalls cater for lovers too, with'constant hearts / Some stuck with comfits, some transfix'd with darts', and the poet turns his gaze onto the rustic couples:–

'Now Hodge his taste so rare attempts to prove
In fixing on a fairing for his Love,
A token meant to show his truth sincere
A china Box with 'This I give my dear'
A pair of garters or perhaps a ring
No, no, the garters are the very thing,
One pair of azure blue supremely shone
This too their motto 'I love one alone'.
The Money's paid, to Sue again he hies,
Gains one sweet kiss and all the world defies...'

Evidendly when Okeden went, the festive side of the Fair had become as important as its commercial basis. There is other evidence for this. Letitia Clapcott, arrested for telling fortunes at Woodbury in the early 19th century (*DYB* 1981 p22) must have been a fairground entertainer. It was common for townspeople to come out for a days entertainment; in 1786 a Poole diarist made a note of the 'numbers of Carriages out of Town to Woodberey Hill Fair' (DRO: D365/F9).

By the late 18th or 19th century the five days of the Fair had become devoted to different purposes.

The first was Wholesale Day; the second, Gentlefolks Day, when the upper classes would drive here from the country round about to try the amusements. The first roast pork of the season would be for sale, and large numbers of oysters were eaten; and there was 'the shaking of the Country-lads of the neighbourhood into their new leathern breeches by an ancestor of Mr. Rolls, breeches-maker, of Puddletown'. The third day was All folks Day, when the amusements were more popular; the fourth was Sheep-fair Day; and the fifth, Pack-and-Penny Day, when goods were sold cheap by traders getting ready to move on (Pickard-Cambridge 1885).

Throughout its decline, the Fair had loyal supporters. In 1878 an earnest young bicycle enthusiast peddled there to meet friends and relations (*DYB* 1961-2 p125); carters and keepers from surrounding villages would attend it (*DYB* 1953-4 p88; 1961-2 p164); and Olive Knott remembered that in the early decades of this century Mary Ann, the reddle-woman of eastern Dorset,'never missed visiting Woodbury Hill Fair... There she would be seen enjoying all the fun a country fair could offer. Even the helter-skelter had no fears. Down on her mat she would slide, shouting to all and sundry: 'That's it, me dears. Enjoy yerselves while you be young' (*DYB* 1954–5 p148).

Like most folk custom, the history of the Fair can be traced through a stream of criminal proceedings, arising from the fights of holiday-makers, the sharp dealing of stall-holders, or the work of the ubiquitous professional pickpocket. A letter of the early 1600s makes mention of a man brought before the magistrate 'for an affray he made at Woodberry Hill' (DRO: D355/2), and there is a great deal of relevant material in Sir Frances Ashley's casebook (1614-35), the Woodbury entries from which are extracted in *SDNQ* 30 p203, 1976. They show how large an area the traders came from, what sort of accommodation they were put up in, and how business and pleasure were being mixed by the fair-goers. Later, Horace Budden wrote a poem about two hawkers, doubtless apocryphal figures, who tried to overreach each other at the Fair (*DYB* 1938 p82). All this had one lasting consequence. Ralph Wightman – for whom the real Fair had died out in 1914 – wrote in the 60s, 'As little as thirty years ago Bere Regis was regarded as the toughest police beat in Dorset. The reason can only be guessed as the settlement here of some of the extremely tough types from all over England who used to travel from fair to fair' (Wightman 1977 p67). But crime is always an exception, and it is more true to think of the Fair in the words of another poet, William Holloway:–

'Thro' the village last night the strong pack-horses pac'd,
We heard their bells jingle adown the dark lane
The clamorous drovers the roads have retrac'd
And lowings, and bleatings, wide echo'd again...
Come Lucy! Come Hannah! away to the fair –
The booths are erected, the shows are begun
Each maid from the farm and the dairy is there –
Ere the sky-lark ascended, their labours were done'

(Woodbury-Hill, in *Scenes of Youth*, 1803).

There were several permanent or semi-permanent structures built to serve the Fair. Okeden saw them in 1796:.

'And now the distant Booths attract the Eye
Looking like new-wash'd linnen hung to dry
Whilst on their Tops in varied Colours twin'd
The strameing pendant wav'd to every wind'.

In 1688 a rent was agreed on for a copyhold tenement at the Fair (DRO:0320/T86), and the building accounts in the Gould family notebook, kept 1723-1850, frequently record orders for timber-built houses to be put up on the hill, with the names of the traders and the location of their standings given (Pitfield 1978 p91 and DRO:D1/PH2). Taylor's map of 1777 (Pitfield 1978 p28) shows about ten permanent buildings arranged in a street on the hill, and in the great fire of Bere in 1788, the homeless suffers retired for shelter 'to the buildings erected for the fair on Woodbury Hill' (Hutchins): this was on the 4th June, so clearly the buildings must have been left standing all year round. There was a pub on the hill, and in a curious throwback to the beginnings of the fair, services were held when a Sunday intervened between the two days of the Victorian festival, as in 1895, and a schoolroom was improvised for Sunday school. A few years earlier in 1884 an Itinerant Missioner had been busy baptising children (presumably those of the gipsy traders) at the Fair (DRO:PE/BER/RE12). The 1887 OS shows nine permanent buildings lying on either side of the street that runs from north to south, and four others stood at various points on the ramparts. These were probably all built of brick, the same that had housed the displaced people in 1788. Today four of them survive. They are built to a more or less regular plan, as rectangles of about 15 by 35 feet, evidently reflecting the area allotted to each stall. To the west of the street (now used as a farm track) is a farmhouse and two barns or sheds; to the east of it, a shed. The earliest phase of the brickwork is 18th-century, and the barns, as might be expected, are jerry-built: the mortar is very thin, and a succession of buttresses has been needed to keep the fabric upright. No excavation has been done in the fort, which is perhaps unique among its class of monuments in that its historical occupation has been more populous and important then the prehistoric settlement. The only archaeological observation on the debris of so many centuries is Pickard-Cambridge's comment that oyster shells were to be dug up among the old stalls.

Woodhouse Hill   Romano-British settlement   Studland
This is probably the monument referred to, in a very garbled fashion, by Leonard
Tatchell in 1954.
'The beautiful 'Whitecliff House' built in Tudor times on the site of a Roman villa; this
probably gives rise to the legend, that at certain periods, a Roman Captain is seen in the
company of a British Maiden' (Tatchell p88).

Wor Barrow   Long barrow: G.I.   Sixpenny Handley
Wor Barrow is so named on the O.S. (1811). The reference in the *Minute Books of the
Dorset Standing Committee,* in 1546, to 'a place callyd Werebarewe... watch and ward
duty at Warbarrow', are located here by Mills, but may more properly belong to a place on
the coast, Worbarrow Tout or *Werybarowe* in Canford Magna.
A writer from Sixpenny Handley says the monument 'which the villagers called
Playbarrow (its proper name is Worbarrow), was reputed to contain a golden coffin, and
was excavated by the late General Pitt Rivers, though he never found the coffin'. The
barrow is called Pega's barrow in the charter of 956 (*DP* 58 p116, 1936), and Playbarrow
is probably a survival of this original name.
After excavation, Pitt Rivers employed the spoil from the site to construct a concert
grandstand. Such educational philanthropy is typical of the General: it is unlikely that he
would have recognised it as a new form of folklore – a renewal of the ancient custom of
games played on the holy mound.

SITES OF DISPUTED ARCHAEOLOGICAL STATUS

The Devil's Armchair   ? Chambered long barrow   Corscombe
The site is at 513049, on arable land just south of a copppice which is now being partly
built over for a housing estate. It consists of three upright stones, about four or five feet
high, and behind them five more large stones extending in a line. To the south of this group
are two other stones which are clearly too large to have been used in any megalithic
structure. The three upright stones form a crescent shape facing south-east, and the stones
behind them occupy a truncated triangular shape extending along this orientation: but
there roughness of the vegetation makes it impossible to tell whether any slight mound
exists beneath them.
In 1925 Vere Oliver identified this site as a previously unknown chambered long
barrow, presumably basing this conclusion on the long shape, orientation, and apparent
crescentic forecourt formed by the upright stones, all of which are analogous to the Grey
Mare at Longbredy. The Royal Commission have scheduled the site as 'three standing
stones'. More recently, the Sarsen Survey of the Society of Antiquaries has passed a
motion 'to determine whether a sarsen standing upright in the Fuller's Earth at Corscombe
is naturally so or not'.
The site 'has the local name of 'The Devil's Armchair' '(*DP* 46 p.1xv, 1925) – the
upright stones look something like a chair, though they do not make as easy a seat as the
Devil's Chair in the Avebury avenue. The Sarsen Survey refers to it as 'Granny's
Armchair', but this may be a variant or an error. When I asked about the site in
Corscombe, I inquired first for the standing stones and then for the Devil's Armchair, and
this second name was immediately recognised.

The site is at the bottom of a valley, and at least two stones near it are natural sarsens. The upright stones must have been so placed by human agency; their location in low ground and on Fuller's Earth argue against a prehistoric origin, but the appearance of the monument itself suggests otherwise.

The Devil's Stone ? Megalith Bere Regis/Turnerspuddle

The Devil's Stone on Black Hill is a sarsen, about four feet high and evidently set upright by human agency.It stands at the crossing of two paths over the heath on a small rise of ground (not a barrow, despite Pitfield 1978 p8) and lies on the boundary of Bere and Turnerspuddle. It appears on the 1888 O.S. which marks it as a boundstone, but there is no need for such a stone at the site. There are three barrows on the other side of the track.

The name Devil Stone is applied to a natural rock outcrop near Portesham Withy Beds, and is used for stones and sarsens in other counties, as at Staple Fitzpaine and Churchstanton in Somerset, and Hemyock in Devon.

The Hellstone as it was before an attempted restoration in 1866; an engraving from the first edition of Hutchins, 1774.

Littlemayne   ? Stone circle   West Knighton

Before its destruction, this site was described as a large and complex group of megaliths; afterwards, as a random collection of sarsens. The documentary evidence is set out in Hutchins and *DP* 30 (1909), in which a map is given of the then surviving stones. The Royal Commission assume that they are only sarsens, but since that time short excavations at Broadmayne have revealed Beaker burials (*DP* 88p 103, 1966; 95 p44, 1973). The stones are clearly sarsens in origin, for fresh ones have been turned up by the plough or found during building work in recent years; but the names of Broadmayne, Friarmayne and Littlemayne (from Celtic *maen*, 'stone') show at least that they existed as a landmark in the 11th century. The proximity of the Beaker burials suggests that this natural monument may have been used as a cult site.

The stones 'were called locally the Littlemayne Rocks. An old lady, who used as a girl to come out and play among them, told him that one large stone was called 'the giant without a head' (*DP* 30 p.xlvi, 1909). This anthropomorphic stone sounds like an earlier, lost feature of the site, recorded by Roger Gale in 1710. 'The stones were very large and rude. I saw the remains of one that had been hollowed... and had been about six feet deep, as I was told by Mr. Conyers Place, who saw it entire. Before it stood, as he assured me, two small images about three feet high, resembling children in swaddling clothes, and of rude work' (Hutchins 1861-70 2p 502).

The Sliding Stone   ? Megalith   Bettiscombe

On Sliding Hill a stone four feet high, and some seven inches wide and three inches thick, was identified as a megalith by the Ordnance Survey in 1887; it has subsequently disappeared. There is also a sarsen which stands alone at the northern foot of Sliding Hill; it is nine feet high and some seven feet wide (see a discussion by Major Tylor, O.S. Crawford, and Vere Oliver in *SDNQ* 19 p131, 153, 213 and 205). In confusion, the designation of 'standing stone' has been transferred from the first to the second site.

It is now said that Sliding Hill is so named because halfway up is a Wishing Stone which rolls down the hill on Midsummer Eve and up again the next day (Turner 1973 p138).

HAUNTED ANCIENT ROADS

I have grouped these cases together, since they have stonger links with each other than with the other sites in the Inventory. The road is, next to the pub and the stately home, one of the most common places for ghost traditions and sightings. Most of the stories are attached to local or disused tracks, and one of the social functions of the stories is to keep alive the memory of old roads: but it is rare for ghosts to appear on roads of very ancient date. The exception is the coastal ridgeway from Abbotsbury to Swanage, which has a remarkable sequence of hauntings throughout its length. In addition, there have been various apparitions of marching soldiers, chiefly Roman, and one prehistoric ghost.

The Roman road which runs from Dorchester to Eggardon 'was built by the Devil in one night' (Waring 1977 p34). According to an informant in 1983, you see Roman soldiers on the stretch that runs past Compton Valence. It was probably along this road that a phantom army was seen in 1662. 'Upon the 29th of June, a reverend and godly Minister, one of the King's chaplains, as he was travelling with his man between Winterbourne [ie. Abbas] and Dorchester, saw a great troop of horses upon the top of a hill with colours flying, some of them alighted and walked down the hill: his man also saw the same, and did both really believe that they were a troop of horse, in as much, that they put on and rode hard, that they might get into Dorchester before the horsemen, to provide themselves of convenient quarters. But they still expecting when the troop should come, and none coming, upon enquiry found that there were really no horsemen thereabouts that day' (The *Annus Mirabilis* tracts, quoted in *SDNQ* 4p 297, 1894).

There is a story that while being driven from Bradford Peverell to Muckleford (a route which would use the Roman road that links Dorchester and Ilchester) a coach overturned into a bog by the roadside and the driver and horses were killed. 'The apparition of the coach being driven by the coachman is supposed to be seen at midnight. About fifty years ago parents of Muckleford children would not allow the children to pass the spot where the mishap occurred, but sent them to Stratton School on the main road instead' (*DYB* 1943–4 p48).

Wilkinson Sherren tells a story of a farmer who lived 'in a village five miles from Dorchester... When returning home from market one evening, through a meadow amid hills crowned with Celtic barrows, the old man said he heard strains of faint music, and saw the ground around him covered with battalions of phantoms, wheeling, advancing, and retiring as if engaged in battle'. The farmer was 'one of the old school, close-lipped, superstitious, and a pillar of the local chapel (Sherren 1902 p 24). The village (one of the Winterbornes?) cannot be identified, but this phantom army is clearly analogous to the other hauntings.

In the autumn of 1969, the figure of a Roman soldier was seen in the woods at Thorncombe, in Stinsford, by fourteen people. A dozen boys from Guy's Marsh Borstal, at Shaftesbury, had established a working camp, under the supervision of two adults: although they were not aware of it at the time, the camp stood on the line of the Dorchester-Badbury Roman road. In the evening of the 13th October, a boy rushed into the camp, talking about the ghost he had seen in the trees – a figure with a sword and shield, wearing a toga (sic) and a helmet. The others in the camp went to investigate, and saw the apparition, until one of the staff approached it with a torch, when it disappeared. The figure was seen at some height above the ground, and was supposed to be standing on the old road level (Legg 1974 p37).

I have heard (1985) accounts of Roman soldiers seen on the Dorchester-Weymouth road by Winterborne Monkton, and on the old Sherborne road from Dorchester, up at Dogbury Gate.

The prehistoric ghost seen by Dr. R. C. C. Clay was a unique apparition. The account has been published in two sources (Grinsell 1952 p57, and Day 1958 p14), which differ only in minor changes of wording. Dr. Clay was driving from Cranborne to Handley in the winter of 1927-8, and 'had reached the spot between the small clump of beeches on the east and the pinewood on the west where the road dips before rising to cross the Roman Road' – about 020158, at or just before the Dorset Cursus – when he saw a horseman on the downs, going the same way as himself. 'Suddenly he turned his horse's head and galloped as if to reach the road ahead , before my car arrived there. I was so interested that I changed gear to slow my car's speed in order that we should meet, and I should be able to find out why he had taken this sudden action. Before I had drawn level with him, he turned his horse's head again to the north, and galloped along parallel to me about fifty yards from the road. I could now see that he was no ordinary horseman, for he had bare legs, and wore a long, loose coat. The horse had a long mane and tail, but I could see no bridle or stirrups. The rider's face was turned toward me, but I could not see his features. He seemed to be threatening me with some implement which he waved in his right hand above his head. I tried hard to identify the weapon, for I suddenly realised that he was a prehistoric man; but I failed. It seemed to be on a two-foot shaft. After travelling parallel to my car for about 100 yards, the rider and horse suddenly vanished. I noted the spot, and the next day found at this spot a low round barrow'. Grinsell gives other reports of a phantom horseman on Bottlebrush Down (1952 p57). Aubrey Parke has only a brief mention for the 'story that the Rev. A. R. T. Bruce was chased off Oakley Down by a ghostly warrior because, when I asked him if this adventure had indeed occurred, he denied it, albeit regretfully' (Parke 1963 p483). This may be a confused idea of Clay's sighting.

The Ridgeway hauntings are remarkable for their geographical extension along the line of a prehistoric road. According to the analysis in Ronald Good's *Old Roads of Dorset* the Ridgeway effectively begins at Abbotsbury Castle; it runs along White Hill, over Blackdown, along the hill north of Corton Down, then crosses the Roman road at Ridgeway cutting, proceeds past Came Wood, along White Horse Hill to Poxwell, and moving towards the coast runs past Bindon and Flowers Barrow, along Whiteway Hill and the Purbeck Ridge past Corfe, ending at Ballard Down.

The first hauntings are mentioned at Abbotsbury. According to an informant in Grinsell 1952 p56, 'he was told that if he sat on the gate near New Barn at midnight, he would see the ghosts of the soldiers who were buried there': and I have been told that an army can be seen marching up the hill. The next point is at Ridgeway tunnel: 'Roman armies... march above Weymouth, and also in Purbeck in times of national emergency' (Waring 1977 p81). An informant told me that she had seen, or half-seen, a man riding a horse who then disappeared, on the A354 climbing Ridgeway Hill. She was inclined afterwards to think it was a trick of the light. Further to the south, a Roman solder is said to appear at the corner where the road to Buckland Ripers turns off the A354 (both items collected 1983).

Next along the Ridgeway comes the group of four singing barrows, described in the Inventory under the headings of Bincombe 5, Culliford Tree, Whitcombe 1, and Winterborne Came barrow. These sites are all in the immediate area of the Ridgeway, and the singular fact of their proximity is accentuated by the absence of any other barrows with similar traditions in the rest of Dorset.

At Bindon we enter the territory of the Lulworth phantom army. There are two primary sources for this, apparently independent and written in consecutive years – 1935 and 1936. 'Just recently an officer told me quite seriously that he could vouch for the fact that on certain nights a phantom Roman army marches along Bindon Hill to their camp on Rings Hill. The thud of the trampling of horses and men is plainly heard, and their indistinct forms seen as the fog drifts. On those nights no rabbits run and no dog will go near' (Loader 1935 p18). This account, coming from members of the Lulworth WI, can be taken as representing local belief, and has been frequently repeated since it was republished by Dacombe.

The second source is less reliable, being a chatty guide to country motoring written in 1936. The author reports various conversations with local characters at each site visited, and these owe something at least to authorial invention. His Wareham informant is reported as saying, 'My cousin – a most level-headed chap – was found raving at the foot of Flowers Barrow last month, saying that he had seen an army of skin-clad folk coming down from the barrow... Everyone knows that a captain and four others, while out clay-cutting, over a hundred years ago, saw an army coming down from the same barrow' (Jenkinson 1936 p36). There is another account, dated August 1940, from a man who heard marching feet as he walked home along the Ridgeway, and stood back to let an invisible host go by 'in silence except for the measured tread, a slight metallic noise, and an occasional muffled cough' (*DYB* 1959-60 p133; it is not made clear whether this is a fictional account, however).

There are later references to the haunting but they are vague and may simply be embroideries of what has been said before. We are told of 'queer unidentifiable noises' at Flowers Barrow: 'now and again strange music; faint calling voices, very faintly heard during a lull in the Channel breezes; vague greyish phantoms, momentarily glimpsed before dissolving into cloud wreaths as they crowded about the cliff edge' (Collman 1975 p26). The army marches 'especially when the current world is at war. People say that it exists, or that it is possible to uncomfortably feel an inexplicable presence' (Legg 1974). The army is said to have been seen in West Lulworth and Church Knowle in 1939, during the War, and in 1970 (*Reader's Digest Book of Folklore* p158), but I have not been able to confirm these references.

The classic story of a phantom armey in Dorset is that of Creech Grange. In 1678, at a spot which is about 910.817: 'one evening, in December, was imagined to be seen a vast number of armed men, several thousands, marching from Flowers Barrow, over Grange Hill; and a great noise and clashing of arms was supposed to have been heard. Nothing appeared on the south side of the hill. They were pretended to have been seen by Capt. John Lawrence, then owner of Grange, who lived there, and his brother, and 100 more, particularly by four clay-cutters, just going to leave off work; and all the people in the cottages and hamlets thereabout, who left their supper and houses, and came to Wareham, and alarmed the town' (Hutchins 1774 1p 206). This account can now be confirmed by a letter from Jane Culliford of Tyneham to her husband Robert, in November 1678: 'My sonne Lawrence Culliford went yesterday & spake with six persons yt were eye witnesses of the numerous appearance on Grange Hill... There was a visible appearance of horsemen & Foote to a great number upon Grange Hill... they being seen between two risings of ye Hill where few bushes were and soe open yt a Crow may be senn' (*SDNQ* p13, 1968).

Finally come the apparitions listed in the Inventory at Kingston Down and Wilkswood, the 'army which marches along the old Priest's Track to Swanage... known to people at Langton and Worth Matravers' (Waring 1977 p81), and, overlooking the sea, the place somewhere near Woodhouse Hill where the Roman centurion and the British girl walk together for ever.

ECCENTRIC AND ALTERNATIVE ARCHAEOLOGY

If the roots of archaeology are bound up with folklore, its development has been as closely intertwined with a tradition of rival theories, variously called pseudo-science by their opponents and alternative archaeology by their supporters. The definition of this tradition is not fixed, since an old othodoxy is liable, with hindsight, to find itself classed as superstition; it happened with Druids, and with diffusion, and will doubtless happen again. But the alternative tradition has an unifying thread, and one which ensures its continuing popularity, even though it may have less access to the media than does orthodoxy. It relies on legendary and symbolical thinking, not just for subject matter, but for the whole mystical atmosphere in which its researchers have worked. In this respect, orthodox and alternative archaeology are locked in an endless marriage of incomprehension, each unable to enter into the thoughts of the other. Perhaps folklore can hold the balance between rationalism and symbolism.

The history of divided attitudes begins with Aubrey and Stukeley, the *Templa Druidum* of the 1690s and *Stonehenge A Temple Restored to the British Druids* of 1740. This association of Druids with ancient monuments was taken from folklore (principally that of Wales), but returned with interest, and in Dorset its influence can be traced from Stukeley's time onwards. Hutchins corresponded with him, giving information on the Cerne Giant, in 1764, and received an interpretation of that figure via the minutes of the Society of Antiquaries the next year. We learn that the Giant was cut in compliment to Eli the father of Caswallawn, in honour of his expelling the Belgae, and that 'unquestionably it means to represent the famous and first Hercules, the Phoenician leader of the first colony to Britain, who came hither for the Cornish tin. It is not to be supposed that it was made in his time, but afterwards, and in memory of him, when the Britons had a notion of the latter Theban Hercules'. Stukeley regards the Phoenicio-British of Dorset as identical to the 'blameless Ethiopians' amongst whom Homer's gods take their rest. 'By Ethiopia, we know well, the ancients meant Arabia, and from Arabia our first Britons came, and were of the same patriarchal religion as those Arabian magi, properly Druids, who came to worship our infant Saviour'. In our own century, A.C. Benson in *The Thread of Gold* was still ornamenting the Giant with Druid horror: 'it seems certainly to be one of the frightful figures of which Caesar speaks, on which captives were bound with twisted osiers and burned to death for a Druidical sacrifice'. As we shall see, the Giant has been a kindly host to every eccentric theory from the 18th century to our own.

Hutchins took note of Stukeley's ideas, and the Kingston Russell stone circle and Agglestone duly appear in the *History* as Druidical monuments. (The Agglestone, although allowed to be natural, was still holding onto its Druids when the *Purbeck Papers* (p80, 1856) were compiled). By Warne's time, the Druid theory had entered popular imagination enough for him to take the local designation of Poxwell as a Druidical circle, as evidence for its antiquity. But the belief has given rise to little folklore, existing only in occasional references. At Badbury 'legend says here the Druids performed and worshipped with strange rites' (Tatchell 1954 p161: and see also Wilks). They are also located at the venerable and sinister yew wood below Hod Hill. The most curious monument they have annexed is the old churchyard cross at Milton Abbas, known in 1903 as The Druid's Cross (*DP* 25p 4). But the *locus classicus* for druidlore in Dorset is not from tradition but the wild and imaginative prose of that soi-disant modern genious, J.F. Pennie. He was a man who had real gifts, unfortunately not including that of making a living. His descriptions of the folk customs in his native East Lulworth are full of observation; and the archaeological passages in his life include an accurate description of the settlement earthworks at Kingston Russell, a discovery in which he was followed by Warne; he was apparently the first to make a cultural comparison between Maori *pahs* and the hillforts of Wessex. But a fit of poetry could always overwhelm his description of antiquities, and at Poxwell (which, to add insult to injury, is not even a stone circle) he looked up from the stones and saw 'the noble prospects of the ancient Druids, as they ascended from their ample and sacred groves of oak, in the valley beneath, to this lofty temple of rocks. The eastern brow of this hill bears evident marks from the earth-works, inequalities of the ground, and number of excavations, to have been the residence of the Druids, the Druidesses, the Bards, and the Ovates, and their attendants, who ministered at the holy place of divination and sacrifice. How often has the philosophic Druid paced to and fro this shadowy avenue of wide rocks, wrapped in solemn meditations on the worship of the gods, or gazed from the sacred circle, with upturned eye, on the moon, as in the

'A Celtic Temple at Winterburn': the Nine Stones, as sketched by William Stukeley in 1723 for the *Itinerarium Curiosum*. He viewed them from the south, whereas a modern traveller will see them on the other side, from the road.

plenitude of her glory the star-crowned pilgrim sowed the waving ocean with beamy gold... Then was heard in the valley below, amid his oaken bower, entwined with the balmy honeysuckle, the wild harp of the young initiated bard...

'It is probable, from the smallness of the inner circle on this hill, and there being no altar or cromlech near, that the wicker image of gigantic proportions, in which were enclosed a number of captives, destined to feed the devouring flames, has been often erected on this spot. And hither to these dreadful sacrifices, and other mysterious rites of blood, at which Pliny says, lib. 22 cap. 2, the British women went naked, but stained dark like the Aethiopians by a vegetable juice, resorted the Celtic population from all the neighbouring settlements – the fierce hordes who wandered with their cattle from place to place, and the warlike denizens of the invincible and once mighty city of Dunium or Maiden Castle' (Pennie 1827 2p 77).

It is almost a textbook case of Druid mania. The two attitudes of reverence and horror

(Stuart Piggott's 'soft primitivism' and 'hard primitivism') glide into one another, as they do in that earlier and greater meditation on megaliths, the Druidic vision in Wordsworth's *Prelude*.

A lesser contemporary of the Druid theories was the Arkite system, which held that all mythologies were derived from an original set of beliefs devised by Noah's immediate descendants as grateful metaphors for their salvation in the Ark. The urge to find a common origin for all mythology, which continues to inspire modern researchers, is a curiously addictive pursuit. To say that all legends take their rise from a single authoritative source is one way, in a secular age, of affirming the reality of myth. There were Arkite interpretations of Shipton Hill (Warne 1872 p96), which of course looked acceptably like a beached ship; and this explanation was extended to Maiden Castle. 'Like its sister mount, or caph, in the isle of Purbeck (now called Corfe Castle), it had its orgin in the religion and worship of the earliest ages, when the Arkite rites were universally practised in both hemispheres... The *mystic* name of Noah was Merd-din (which means 'dweller in the sea') and this island was familiarly called the Garden of Merd-din... Maiden Castle was unquestionably a great Puratheia, or mount dedicated to fire worship, whose name should therefore be Merd-din Caph, or the Mount of Noah; and the circle of small tumuli around it, more decidedly confirms its ancient dedication to the Helio-Arkite Deity, since it plainly represents the well-known Ring of Baal' *(Gentleman's Magazine* 96p 258, 1826). The belief that all ancient monuments have a religious import is another recurrent theory in alternative archaeology.

One theory which nearly achieved orthodoxy was that of Phoenicians along the Dorset coast. Only Warne's authority consigned them to the realms of myth, although they continued to make fugitive appearances in the early numbers of *Dorset Proceedings*. Pennie espoused them with customary fervour, writing to the *Poole and Dorsetshire Herald* (June 1847) about Bindon Hill. 'We believe these ramparts to have been the defensive works of the Phoenicians. On what grounds? First, not only from situation, but their stone walls, singular outer-stations and circular *towers*. Secondly, from a discovery made some years since... of a settlement for traffic of the same people in the neighbouring Isle of Purbeck, and more than all, from the name it bears, *Bhin* in the Phoenician language, signifying a lofty eminence, while *don* in Celtic is the term for a fortress, the same as *dun* in the Scythian'. The discovery referred to is that by William Miles of some Kimmeridge coal money, imputed by him to a Carthaginian trading community. He argued (1826 p46) that the resemblance of the lathe chucks to coins was evidence of Semitic meanness; the Phoenicians were fobbing off their god with counterfeit coins instead of the real metal. A zeal for etymology appears in a local history of Weymouth: 'Faber in his 'Mysteries of the Cabiri', roundly asserts Melcombe to be a Phoenician word, and brings authorities from various quarters... There are also some tumuli near Lulworth, which are called Yules Kitchen, which is a corruption of Kist-vaen, a stone chest, typical of the ark, and here the priest of the Helio-Arkite deity, performed his mystic rites; Yule is the vestige of the festival of the winter solstice, and signifies a turning or revolution, where the votaries of fire worship rolled an ignited wheel enveloped in tow &c. down the hill'. Further philologies include: 'Kumar, and the Saxon, ridge, Kimmeridge, a land of uneven surface; Pur-bec, the house of fire, or seat of the sun; Caph-Corfe, a mount dedicated to fire-worship; and the word Coal money is probably derived from Cal-Col, or Cala, confined or enclosed'. (Ellis 1829 p106).

After Kimmeridge coal money received a more prosaic interpretation, Dorset's

Phoenicians went into obscurity, only to be retrieved in the next century when British Israelitism was added to the heady brew. Comyns Beaumont (1945 p115) undertook the task of identifying Britain (mainly Wessex and the Hebrides) with the Holy Land of the Scriptures, and Dorset caught his eye. 'Those who study the remarkable antiquities of Portland and Melcombe Regis adjoining that rocky peninsula may find affinities with the city of Tyre as historically described. Portland was an almost impregnable fortress in olden days, separated from the mainland by a channel. It recalls the tremendous siege of Alexander the Great... It appears that at the time of the Flood it was destroyed by earthquake and submerged for about seventy years... Portland, among its strange possessions, produces fossilised trees, sure sign of a tremendous visitation, and ancient underground chambers, found in 1880, of the beehive type. Early fibulae, pottery, and stone sarcophagi have been found... The Pulpit Rock, at the southern extremity, called Portland Bill, really the Beale, which recalls the saying of Ezekiel, of the ruler of Tyre, 'Thou said, 'I am a God, I sit in the seat of God in the midst of the seas'. The name Beale appears to be derived from Baal or Bel' (Beaumont 1945 p115). Like the rest, the Phoenicians have been discovered at Cerne *(Country Life* 18 Oct. 1924).

Geoffrey of Monmouth could be seen as an early alternative archaeologist – more so, at least, than an historian – so it is natural to find him being adopted in some 19th-century theories. This time, Portland is the Totnes where Brut the Trojan landed and began to subdue the savage giants of Albion. Brut's right-hand-man Corineus was, we read, a great wrestler, and by single combat in that art defeated Goemagot, the last of the giants. One H.F. Napper interpreted the Cerne Giant as a memorial to this vanquished Goemagot, and derived 'Cerne' itself from Corineus. (*SDNQ* 1p 140, 1888).

In the giometrical schemes of W.H. Black, the Giant assumes a pivotal role. A line drawn from him to the Whiteleaf Cross in Buckinghamshire will extend to Ushant one way, and on the other to the middle point of the Wash; and a line from St. Catherine's Chapel (Abbotsbury) through the Giant also strikes Happisburg in Norfolk, allegedly a Roman site. *(J. of the Brit. Arch. Assoc.* 28p 234, 1972). The orientations are accurate, whatever their value as evidence for the Roman scheme of land measurement to which Black devoted his energies. He calculates the metrology of the Giant, supposing the 60 ft. unit of Hutchins' rough measurements to be a clue for an equal number of geographical miles, and on this basis detects Roman agrimensors at work in Kit's Coty House and Berwick-Tweed.

From Black it is an easy step to Alfred Watkins, who was first inspired with the linear vision by hearing the former lecturing at Hereford, and whose ley theory forms the matrix of modern alternative archaeology. In the following notes leys will be discussed without value judgements or controversy; they have a symbolic importance in popular culture, and that is enough. It would of course be absurd to consider the whole subject as a branch of folklore, for it is an independent discipline with its own debates, journals, researches, and developments, but its folkloristic aspects form an impartial meeting-ground for geomancers and archaeologists. There is a need for some such common ground: it is absurd that two sets of researchers with common needs and interests in preserving the ancient landscape should engage in a perpetual cold war.

Apart from some placename speculations (the work of a gazetteer rather than local knowledge) and observations on barrow alignments at Badbury and Knowlton, there are only two Dorset items in *The Old Straight Track*. One (p104) is a revision of earlier research. Sir Norman Lockyer had identified a ley running through Stonehenge, from Grovely Castle to Sidbury and Winterborne Camps. Watkins proposed a southern extension through Cerne Abbas to Puncknowle Beacon. In the present system of nomenclature (southernmost parish + orientation) this would alter it from *Great Wishford 53* to *Puncknowle 53*. But as the line crosses all of O.S. sheet 194 without touching on anything but the beacon barrow on Puncknowle Hill and the obligatory Cerne Giant, we may as well leave it unrevised.

The other ley (p190), on a probable reconstruction from his brief description, would be *Bincombe 331*. It runs from the eastern edge of Chalbury, through the barrow Bincombe 35, then one of the Came Down group, Winterborne Herringston 3, Maiden Castle (at the point where the long mound crosses the causewayed camp), Winterborne St. Martin 23, one of the Seven Barrows in Bradford Peverell, and so to the barrow Bradford Peverell 7 on Penn Hill.

In *The View Over Atlantis*, the work that re-introduced Watkins' ideas into the mainstream of geomantic thinking, John Michell proposed a couple of leys across the Vale of Blackmore, *West Compton 56* and *Toller Porcorum 61*. Both of these consist of churches only, being introduced as proof for site continuity between prehistoric and Christian sites: but meeting at Child Okeford church, both proceed to graze the northern ramparts of Hambledon Hill. Michell's leys were republished in *Dorset Countryside* 1vii p32, 1976. He wrote a straightforward article advancing the neo-Watkinsian viewpoint, with no additional Dorset material except in the illustrations, which show St. Peter's at Church Knowle 'on a mound within the remains of a circular churchyard', a suggested case of site continuity; a sarsen or markstone by the crossroads at Littlebredy; and a green road, thought to be an ancient trackway, at Lydlinch – three sites which would repay fieldwork. The article was followed by a brisk discussion pro and anti in the Letters page. Michell's leys also inspired a rather garbled passage in *Arcana,* a Cambridge publication. 'Salisbury Cathedral... is on a direct alignment to Child Okeford in Dorset, situated beneath the prehistoric earthworks of Hambledon Hill, a notable centre for old tracks and lines of churches... Hambledon Hill is in direct line with Glastonbury and passes by South Cadbury' (Aug. 1973 p31).

The number of published Dorset leys is quite small: only ten have been individually studied. The suggestion, originally made by Allcroft, that the three barrows to the west of the Knowlton-Wimborne road were positioned to align onto the main henge there is taken up by Allen Cooper (DYB 1973-4 p25), and developed into a ley *Woodlands 25,* to which he adds lines at 332° and 342° through the henge and church, which may be intended for leys. The article notes that the 25° orientation corresponds to the Avenue at Stonehenge, and quotes some unpublished observations by Lyle Borst on triangles that can be laid out in megalithic yards to define the dimensions of Knowlton church and its enclosing henge.

A discussion on the folklore of Culpepper's Dish in *Dorset* 29p 32, 1973, elicited the following ley *(Arne 303)* from R.H. Manley; it begins at a round barrow (Grinsell's Arne 16) and in its north-west course runs through Culpepper's Dish, four more barrows, and three sets of earthworks, ending at a crossroads in Melbury Osmond.

Two leys have been proposed as passing through the golf course at Came Down. One, *Owermoigne 270,* starts at tinkers Barrow (G.1) in Owermoigne, and runs through West Knighton 2, Winterborne St. Martin 45, Winterborne Steepleton 38, Kingston Russel stone circle, and Puncknowle 1. The other, *Wool 270,* starts at the crossroads of Burton Cross and runs through Wool 4, Winfrith 7, Whitcombe 7, Whitcombe Came 4, and three large barrow groups – the first on Ridgeway Hill, the others on White and Wears Hills in Abbotsbury. Both leys are the work of the historian of the golf course, where it is interesting to find that some of the holes are laid out in minature alignments in the barrows of the Down (Ward 1984 p27).

The town historian of Bridport has proposed a short alignment comprising Thorncombe Beacon, St. Mary's church, and Boarsbarrow Hill; he supports it by evidence of aligned tracks (Short 1980 p11).

A ley, *East Lulworth 292,* has been proposed by Barry Chilvers to explain the car breakdowns at the Nine Stones and Monkton Hill. Making sense of the newspaper report, it can be identified as running from Flowers Barrow through the barrow Winterborne Came 34, past the south-western tip of Maiden Castle, through Martinstown church and the Nine Stones, to the barrow Winterbourne Abbas 11. It passes through the sites of both car breakdowns, but not, despite what the Echo says, through Eggardon or Pilsdon *(Dorset Evening Echo* 26 Jan. 1985).

Francis Hitching in his *World Atlas of Mysteries* cites a west Dorset ley given him by a 'West Country archaeologist'. This authority is quoted as having identified the Iron-Age rectangular structure from the Pilsdon excavations as a Bronze-Age ceremonial path; I do not think he will be found in the universities. The ley *(Whitchurch Canonicorum 47)* begins at Coney's Castle, runs through Bettiscombe church, up a track to the Manor with its celebrated screaming skull, through a 'standing stone' (rock outcrop) on Sliding Hill, over Pilsdon, crosses old fords at Burstock and Mosterton, and ends in a church surrounded by medieval earthworks at South Perrott. With eight points in about a dozen miles it is the most compact alignment so far.

The ruins of Corfe Castle, 'an unforgettable sight' for Paul Devereux of *The Ley Hunter,* seen here in an engraving made for the early 19th century tourist market.

The pick of Dorset leys are represented by the three examples given in Devereux & Thomson (1979 p107). Their work shows careful surveying, fieldwalking, and archival research; on certain points (for instance, the barrow West Knighton 3, rather attractively made into a garden feature) they are able to correct the Ordnance Survey. The leys are measured with accuracy that can take account of yards.

The first – *Corfe Castle 93*, in their system SW1 – runs through a group of Purbeck barrows; West Lulworth 10, Tyneham 19, 11, Steeple 1, and Church Knowle 8 – 'a public footpath from the road past Church Knowle leads up directly to this round barrow, which can be seen etched dramatically against the skyline. A walk along the ridge of the Purbecks down the ley from the tumulus soon reveals the unforgettable sight of ruined Corfe Castle'. From the Castle, whose headless ghost is duly noted, the ley proceeds to end at Rempstone stone circle. In addition to the points observed by Devereux and Thomson, it has passed near the lost site of East Lulworth stone circle and the place where the Creech Grange army was seen; it corresponds in part at least with the accepted Ridgeway.

The second ley – *Warmwell 108* (SW2) begins by grazing the north-east corner of Warmwell church; from there to the barrow West Knighton 3, thence over the site of Littlemayne stone circle (though they do not mention this), through Broadmayne church, along the north bank of Maiden Castle, through the ploughed-out long barrow Winterbourne Monkton I, and ending at the pair of barrows Winterbourne Steepleton 3 and 4. This ley has been the subject of special criticism from Williamson and Bellamy (1983 p140) who point out that it passes through the final Iron Age phase of Maiden Castle and not the earlier Neolithic work. The criticism is only valid in terms of Devereux' own explanation of mixed-marker leys as the result of site continuity; other theorists assume that they are the product of an innate human tendency to generate alignments of sites.

Their third ley relies on the ubiquitous Cerne Giant: *Cerne Abbas 17* (SW3). Starting at Holwell church, it runs through the barrow Buckland Newton 3, a settlement at 669.021, the problematical Trendle, the remains of Cerne Abbey, St. Augustine's Well, and finally the church of St. Mary in Cerne.

So ends a short excursus into the back streets of archaeological theory. What is clear from a brief summary of these theories of three centuries is their separateness from orthodox thinking, and their latent influence on cultural values and folklore. The geomantic tradition depends on standards of philology, statistics, and associative thinking which repel orthodoxy; but it is in its own way a reflection of the elusive symbolic worldview which underlies religious thinking and created the most prominent monuments of the past. Stonehenge may be studied by reason, but it was created by faith. Modern legends as well as ancient monuments are the work of human creativity, and by picking up the clues of folklore we are able to follow the ways of the human mind.

Allcroft, A. Hadrian, 1908 — *Earthwork of England.*

Anderson, O. S., 1939 — 'The English Hundred names: the South-Western counties'; *Acta Universitatis Lundensis* 35p235-285,

Aubrey, John, 1687 — *Remaines of Gentilisme and Judaisme.* London 1881.
Monumenta Britannica – ed. Legg and Fowles. Dorset Publishing Company 1980 (1665-93).

Bailey, C. J., 1982 — *The Bride Valley.* Dorchester.

Bankes, George, 1853 — *The Story of Corfe Castle.*

Barnes, William, 1962 — *The Poems of William Barnes.*

Bartelot, Richard G., 1915 — *The History of Fordington.* Dorchester.

Beaumont, William Comyns, 1945 — *The Riddle of Prehistoric Britain.*

Benfield, Eric, 1950 — *Dorset.*

Bettey, J. H., 1970 — *The Island and Royal Manor of Portland.* Portland.

Bond, L. M. G., 1956 — *Tyneham, a Lost Heritage.* Dorchester.

Briggs, Katherine M., 1977 — *A Dictionary of Fairies.*

Burne, Charlotte S., and Jackson, Georgina F., 1883 — *Shropshire Folk-lore.*

Calkin, J. Bernard, 1968 — *Ancient Purbeck.* Dorchester.

Camden, William, 1695 — *Britannia* – ed. tr. Edmund Gibson. Newton Abbot 1971.

Chandler, John, 1984 — *The Register of John Chandler* – ed. Timmins. Devizes.

Collman, Morris, 1975 — *Hants. and Dorset Legends and Folklore.* St. Ives.

Cooksey, Alfred J. A., 1975 — *Signal Beacons in Dorset.* Dorchester.

Cutler, Richard, 1865 — *Original Notes on Dorchester and the Durotriges.* Dorchester.

Dacombe, Marianne R., 1935 — *Dorset Up Along and Down Along.* Dorchester.

Darton, J. Harvey, 1935 — *English Fabric.*

Day, James Wentworth, 1958 — *A Ghost-Hunter's Game Book.*

Devereux, Paul, and Thomson, Ian, 1979 — *The Ley Hunter's Companion.*

Dewar, H. S. L., 1968 — *The Giant of Cerne Abbas.* Guernsey.

Dewar, H. S. L., 1977 — 'The Haunting of Culliford Tree'.
The Literary Repository 1. n.p.

Ellis, George A., 1829 — *The History and Antiquities of Weymouth and Melcombe Regis.* Weymouth.

Fägerston, Anton, 1933 — *The Place-Names of Dorset.* Uppsala.

Field, John E., 1913 — *The Myth of the Pent Cuckoo.*

Fuller, Thomas, 1662 — *The Worthies of England.*

Gale, Elizabeth B., 1983 — *Farmers, Fishermen and Flax Spinners.* Burton Bradstock.

Gant, Roland, 1980 — *Dorset Villages.*

Gascoigne, Bamber, 1982 — *Quest for the Golden Hare.*

Gerard, Thomas, 1630 — *The Survey of Dorsetshire.* Milborne Post. 1980.

Goodland, Norman, 1967 — *Sexton's Boy.*

Grinsell, Leslie V., 1952 — *Dorset Barrows.* Dorchester.

     "   " 1982 — *Dorset Barrows Supplement.* Dorchester

     "   " 1976 — *Folklore of Prehistoric Sites in Britain.* Newton Abbot.

Harman, M., Molleson, T. I., and Price, J. L., 1981 — 'Burials, bodies and beheadings in Romano-British and Anglo-Saxon cemeteries'
Bull. Br. Mus. Nat. Hist. (Geol) 35iii p145-188.

Hill, David, and
Metcalfe, D. M., eds., 1984   *Sceattas in England and on the Continent.*
                                     British Archaeological Reports.
Hope, Robert Charles, 1893   *The Legendary Lore of the Holy Wells of England.*
Hoskins, W. G., 1967   *Fieldwork in Local History.*
Howe, Charles, 1983   *Gylla's Hometown.* Gillingham.
Hubbard, Arthur, and George, 1907   *Neolithic Dew-Ponds and Cattle-Ways.*
Hutchins, John, 1774   *The History and Antiquities of Dorset.* 1st edition.
   "   "   1796-1814   "   2nd edition.
   "   "   1861-70   "   3rd edition
Hyams, John, 1970   *Dorset.*
Hyland, Paul, 1978   *Purbeck, the Ingrained Island.*
Jenkinson, A. S., 1936   *In Search of Romantic Britain.*
Johnson, Walter, 1912   *Byways in British Arhaeology.* Cambridge.
Jones, Barbara, 1953   *Follies and Grottoes.*
Jones, Mary D., 1952   *Cerne Abbas*
Knott, Olive, 1976   *Tales of Dorset.* Dorchester.
Lea, Hermann, 1913   *Thomas Hardy's Wessex.*
Legg, Rodney, 1972   *Purbeck Island.* Milborne Port.
Legg, Rodney, et al., 1974   *Ghosts of Dorset, Devon and Somerset.* Milborne Port.
Loader, J. and P., 1935   *Tales of Lulworth in Olden Days.* Poole.
Major, A. F.,
   and Whistler, C., 1913   *Early Wars of Wessex.* Cambridge.
Marnhull . . . by the Marnhull Women's Institute. 1940.
Matthews, F. W., 1923   *Tales of the Blackdown Borderland.* Taunton
Mayo, Charles H., 1908   *The Municipal Records of the Borough of Dorchester.*
                                     Exeter.
Mercer, Roger, 1980   *Hambledon Hill – A Neolithic Landscape.* Edinburgh.
Miles, William A., 1826   *A Description of the Deverel Barrows . . . and
                                       . . . of the Kimmeridge Coal Money.*
Mills, A. D., 1980   *The Place-names of Dorset.* Vols. 1 and 2. Cambridge.
Moule, H. J., 1901   *Dorchester Antiquities.* Dorchester.
Palmer, Kingsley, 1973   *Oral Folk-Tales of Wessex.* Newton Abbot.
Parke, Aubrey L., 1963   'The folklore of Sixpenny Handley, Dorset',
                                       Folklore 74p481-506.
Pennie, J. F., 1827   *The Tale of a Modern Genius.* London.
Pickard-Cambridge, O. W., 1885   'Woodbury Hill' – in, *DP* 7p93.
Piggot, Stuart, 1944   'Excavations of Barrows on Crichel and Launcston Downs,
                                       Dorset'. *Archaeologia* 90.

   "   "   1950   *William Stukeley.* Oxford.
Pike, Muriel, 1980   *The Piddle Valley Book of Country Life.*
Pitfield, F. P., 1978   *The Book of Bere Regis.* Milborne Port.
Pitt-Rivers, Augustus H., 1887-1905 *Excavations in Cranborne Chase.* 1887-1905.
Pitt-Rivers, Michael, 1966   *Dorset.*
Popham, David, 1983   *The Book of Wimborne.* Buckingham.
Read, T. Dayrell, 1947   *The Rise of Wessex.*
Ross, Anne, 1967   *Pagan Celtic Britain.*
'St. Erkenwald' – tr. Brian Stone.
Sherres, Wilkinson, 1902   *The Wessex of Romance.*
Shore, T. W., 1892   *The History of Hampshire and the Isle of Wight.*
Short, Basil, 1980   *The Book of Bridport.* Buckingham.

Simon, John S., 1870 — *Methodism in Dorset.* Weymouth.
Simpson, Jacqueline, 1979 — *The Folklore of the Welsh Border.*
Smith, A. H., 1956 — *English Placename Elements.* Cambridge.
Smith, H. P., 1951 — *The History of the Borough and County of the Town of Poole.* (vol. 2) Poole.
Smith, R. Bosworth, 1909 — *Bird Life and Bird Lore.*
Sumner, Heywood, 1913 — *Ancient Earthworks of Cranborne Chase.* Chiswick.
Sydenham, John, 1839 — *The History of the Town and County of Poole.* Poole.
    ″   ″   nd. 1841 — *Baal Durotrigensis.*
Tatchell, Leonard, 1954 — *The History of Purbeck.* Dorchester.
Tongue, Ruth, 1967 — *Somerset Folklore.*
Turner, James, 1973 — *Ghosts in the South-West.* Newton Abbot.
Turner, M. Lovett, 1947 — *Tales of Old Charmouth.* Lyme Regis.
Udal, John Symonds, 1922 — *Dorsetshire Folk-Lore.* Dorchester.
Wainwright, G. J.,1979 — *Mount Pleasant, Dorset — Excavations 1970-1.*
Waring, Edward, 1977 — *Ghosts and Legends of the Dorset Countryside.* Tisbury.
Ward, Peter, 1984 — *Came Down to Golf.* Ellesborough.
Warne, Charles, 1866 — *Celtic Tumuli of Dorset.*
    ″   ″   1872 — *Ancient Dorset.* Bournemouth.
Watson, E. W., 1890 — *Ashmore.* Gloucester.
Wheeler, R. E. M., 1943 — *Maiden Castle, Dorset.* Oxford.
Wightman, Ralph, 1977 — *Portrait of Dorset.*
Wilks, J. H., 1978 — *Trees of the British Isles in History and Legend.*
Williamson, Tom,
    and Bellamy, Liz, 1983 — *Ley Lines in Question.* Tadworth.
Wright, Thomas, 1861 — *Essays on Archaeological Subjects.*
Young, Ernest W., 1886 — *Dorchester, its Ancient and Modern History.* Dorchester.

Abbreviations

DCC   *The Dorset County Chronicle.*
DCM   The Dorset County Museum.
DNHAS   The Dorset Natural History and Archaeological Society.
DP   *The Proceedings of the Dorset Natural History & Archaeological Society.*
DRO   The Dorset Record Office.
DYB   *The Year Book of the Society of Dorset Men in London.*
SDNQ   *Somerset and Dorset Notes and Queries.*